Introduction

Welcome to **"The ADHD Cookbook for Women: 100+ ADHD Cookbook Recipes for Nourishing Meals"!** This cookbook is a celebration of the power of food to support and enhance the lives of women managing ADHD.

Living with ADHD presents unique challenges, and maintaining a healthy diet can sometimes feel overwhelming amidst the daily demands of life. But fear not! This cookbook is here to provide you with a collection of delicious, nutritious, and easy-to-prepare recipes specifically tailored to support women with ADHD.

In these pages, you'll find a diverse array of recipes designed to nourish both body and mind. From vibrant salads to hearty soups, from comforting stews to innovative stir-fries, each dish has been thoughtfully crafted to provide essential nutrients while satisfying your taste buds.

But this cookbook is more than just a collection of recipes. It's a guide to embracing your ADHD and harnessing its unique strengths in the kitchen. Throughout these pages, you'll find practical tips and strategies to help you navigate the culinary challenges that often accompany ADHD. From organization and time management to mindful eating and self-care, we'll explore how to create a kitchen environment that supports your well-being.

Whether you're a seasoned home cook or just starting out on your culinary journey, "The ADHD Cookbook for Women" is here to inspire and empower you. So grab your apron, sharpen your knives, and get ready to embark on a delicious adventure—one recipe at a time. Let's cook up a storm and nourish both body and soul together!

1. Grilled Salmon with Lemon Herb Butter

Ingredients:

- 4 salmon fillets (about 6 ounces each), skin-on
- Salt and pepper, to taste
- 2 tablespoons olive oil
- For the Lemon Herb Butter:
- 1/4 cup unsalted butter, softened
- Zest of 1 lemon
- 2 tablespoons fresh lemon juice
- 2 tablespoons chopped fresh parsley
- 1 tablespoon chopped fresh dill
- 1 garlic clove, minced
- Salt and pepper, to taste

Instructions:

- Preheat your grill to medium-high heat.

- Pat the salmon fillets dry with paper towels. Season both sides with salt and pepper, then brush them lightly with olive oil.

- In a small bowl, mix together all the ingredients for the lemon herb butter until well combined.

- Place the salmon fillets skin-side down on the preheated grill. Cook for about 4-5 minutes, then carefully flip them over using a spatula.

- Spoon some of the lemon herb butter over the cooked side of the salmon fillets. Continue to grill for another 4-5 minutes, or until the salmon is cooked to your desired doneness and easily flakes with a fork.

- Once the salmon is cooked, remove it from the grill and transfer to a serving platter. Spoon the remaining lemon herb butter over the top of the salmon.

- Serve the grilled salmon with your favorite side dishes and enjoy!

This recipe is straightforward and shouldn't require too much attention to detail, making it suitable for those with ADHD. Enjoy your delicious grilled salmon with lemon herb butter!

2. Quinoa Salad with Roasted Vegetables

Ingredients:
* 1 cup quinoa, rinsed
* 2 cups water or vegetable broth
* 2 cups mixed vegetables (such as bell peppers, zucchini, cherry tomatoes, red onion, etc.), chopped into bite-sized pieces
* 2 tablespoons olive oil
* Salt and pepper, to taste
* 1/4 cup chopped fresh herbs (such as parsley, basil, or cilantro)
* Optional: crumbled feta cheese or toasted nuts/seeds for topping
* For the Dressing:
* 3 tablespoons extra virgin olive oil
* 2 tablespoons balsamic vinegar
* 1 clove garlic, minced
* 1 teaspoon Dijon mustard
* Salt and pepper, to taste

Instructions:
* Preheat your oven to 400Â°F (200Â°C).

* In a saucepan, combine the quinoa and water or vegetable broth. Bring to a boil, then reduce the heat to low, cover, and simmer for about 15-20 minutes, or until the quinoa is cooked and the liquid is absorbed. Remove from heat and let it sit covered for 5 minutes, then fluff with a fork.

* While the quinoa is cooking, spread the chopped vegetables out on a baking sheet. Drizzle with olive oil, season with salt and pepper, and toss to coat evenly. Roast in the preheated oven for 20-25 minutes, or until the vegetables are tender and slightly caramelized, stirring halfway through. In a small bowl, whisk together the ingredients for the dressing until well combined.

* Once the quinoa and vegetables are cooked, transfer them to a large mixing bowl. Add the chopped fresh herbs and drizzle with the dressing. Toss everything together until evenly combined.

* Taste and adjust seasoning as needed. If desired, sprinkle crumbled feta cheese or toasted nuts/seeds on top before serving. Serve the quinoa salad warm or cold, as a side dish or a main course. Enjoy!

This recipe allows for flexibility in vegetable choices and is packed with nutrients from the quinoa and roasted vegetables. It's easy to prepare and can be made in advance, making it suitable for individuals with ADHD.

3. Chicken Stir-Fry with Broccoli and Bell Peppers

Ingredients:
- 1 lb (about 450g) boneless, skinless chicken breasts or thighs, thinly sliced
- 2 tablespoons soy sauce
- 2 tablespoons oyster sauce
- 1 tablespoon cornstarch
- 1 tablespoon sesame oil
- 2 tablespoons vegetable oil, divided
- 2 cups broccoli florets
- 1 bell pepper (any color), thinly sliced
- 3 cloves garlic, minced
- 1 teaspoon grated ginger
- Cooked rice or noodles, for serving

Instructions:

- In a small bowl, mix together the soy sauce, oyster sauce, and cornstarch. Add the sliced chicken to the bowl and toss to coat. Let it marinate for about 10-15 minutes.

- Heat 1 tablespoon of vegetable oil in a large skillet or wok over medium-high heat. Add the marinated chicken and stir-fry for 4-5 minutes, or until cooked through. Remove the chicken from the skillet and set aside.

- In the same skillet, add the remaining tablespoon of vegetable oil. Add the broccoli florets and sliced bell pepper. Stir-fry for 3-4 minutes, or until the vegetables are tender-crisp.

- Add the minced garlic and grated ginger to the skillet with the vegetables. Stir-fry for another 1-2 minutes, or until fragrant.

- Return the cooked chicken to the skillet with the vegetables. Stir everything together and cook for an additional 1-2 minutes to heat through.

- Drizzle the sesame oil over the stir-fry and toss to combine.

- Serve the chicken stir-fry hot over cooked rice or noodles.

This recipe is quick to prepare and doesn't require a lot of attention to detail, making it suitable for individuals with ADHD. Plus, it's a tasty and nutritious meal option!

4. Veggie-loaded Omelette

Ingredients:

- 3 large eggs
- 2 tablespoons milk or water
- Optional Additions:
- Sliced mushrooms
- Diced zucchini
- Chopped broccoli florets
- Diced ham or cooked bacon
- 1 tablespoon olive oil or butter
- 1/4 cup diced onion
- Salt and pepper, to taste
- 1/4 cup diced bell pepper (any color)
- 1/4 cup diced tomatoes
- 1/4 cup chopped spinach or other leafy greens
- 1/4 cup shredded cheese (such as cheddar, mozzarella, or feta)

Instructions:

- In a medium bowl, whisk together the eggs, milk or water, salt, and pepper until well combined. Heat the olive oil or butter in a non-stick skillet over medium heat.

- Add the diced onion and bell pepper to the skillet. Cook for 2-3 minutes, or until the vegetables start to soften.

- Add any additional veggies you're using, such as tomatoes, spinach, mushrooms, zucchini, or broccoli. Cook for another 2-3 minutes, or until the vegetables are tender. Pour the beaten eggs evenly over the cooked vegetables in the skillet.

- Let the eggs cook undisturbed for about 1-2 minutes, then gently lift the edges of the omelette with a spatula and tilt the skillet to let the uncooked eggs flow to the edges.

- Once the omelette is mostly set but still slightly runny on top, sprinkle the shredded cheese evenly over one half of the omelette.

- Use a spatula to fold the other half of the omelette over the cheese-covered half. Press down gently with the spatula to seal.

- Cook for another 1-2 minutes, or until the cheese is melted and the omelette is cooked through to your liking. Slide the omelette onto a plate and serve hot.

This recipe allows for flexibility in vegetable choices and can be customized based on personal preferences. It's a quick and nutritious meal option that's suitable for individuals with ADHD. Enjoy your veggie-loaded omelette!

5. Spaghetti Squash with Marinara Sauce

Ingredients:

- 1 medium spaghetti squash
- 2 tablespoons olive oil
- Salt and pepper, to taste
- 2 cups marinara sauce (homemade or store-bought)
- Grated Parmesan cheese, for serving (optional)
- Chopped fresh basil or parsley, for garnish (optional)

Instructions:

- Preheat your oven to 400Â°F (200Â°C).

- Carefully slice the spaghetti squash in half lengthwise. Use a spoon to scoop out the seeds and stringy pulp from the center of each half.

- Brush the cut sides of the spaghetti squash halves with olive oil and season with salt and pepper.

- Place the squash halves cut side down on a baking sheet lined with parchment paper or aluminum foil.

- Roast the spaghetti squash in the preheated oven for 35-45 minutes, or until the flesh is tender and easily pierced with a fork.

- While the spaghetti squash is roasting, heat the marinara sauce in a saucepan over medium heat until warmed through.

- Once the spaghetti squash is cooked, remove it from the oven and let it cool for a few minutes.

- Use a fork to scrape the flesh of the spaghetti squash into strands. Transfer the strands to a serving dish.

- Pour the warm marinara sauce over the spaghetti squash strands and toss gently to coat.

- Serve the spaghetti squash with marinara sauce hot, topped with grated Parmesan cheese and chopped fresh basil or parsley, if desired.

This recipe is simple to prepare and doesn't require constant attention, making it suitable for individuals with ADHD. It's a healthy and satisfying alternative to traditional pasta dishes. Enjoy your spaghetti squash with marinara sauce!

6. Baked Chicken Parmesan

Ingredients:

* 4 boneless, skinless chicken breasts
* Salt and pepper, to taste
* 1 cup breadcrumbs (you can use store-bought or homemade)
* 1/2 cup grated Parmesan cheese
* 1 teaspoon dried Italian seasoning
* 1/2 teaspoon garlic powder
* 2 large eggs
* 1 cup marinara sauce
* 1 cup shredded mozzarella cheese
* Fresh basil or parsley, chopped, for garnish (optional)

Instructions:

* Preheat your oven to 400Â°F (200Â°C). Grease a baking dish with non-stick cooking spray or olive oil. Season both sides of the chicken breasts with salt and pepper.

* In a shallow dish, combine the breadcrumbs, grated Parmesan cheese, Italian seasoning, and garlic powder. In another shallow dish, whisk the eggs.

* Dip each chicken breast into the beaten eggs, then coat it with the breadcrumb mixture, pressing gently to adhere. Place the coated chicken breasts in the prepared baking dish.

* Bake the chicken in the preheated oven for 20-25 minutes, or until cooked through and golden brown.

* Remove the baking dish from the oven and spoon marinara sauce over each chicken breast.

* Sprinkle shredded mozzarella cheese evenly over the top of each chicken breast.

* Return the baking dish to the oven and bake for an additional 5-10 minutes, or until the cheese is melted and bubbly.

* Remove the chicken Parmesan from the oven and let it cool for a few minutes.

* Garnish with chopped fresh basil or parsley, if desired, before serving.

This recipe simplifies the traditional chicken Parmesan method by baking instead of frying the chicken, which reduces the hands-on time and cleanup. It's a delicious and comforting meal that's suitable for individuals with ADHD. Enjoy your baked chicken Parmesan!

7. Tofu Stir-Fry with Bok Choy

Ingredients:
- 1 block (14-16 oz) firm tofu, drained and cubed
- 2 tablespoons soy sauce
- 1 tablespoon hoisin sauce
- 1 tablespoon sesame oil
- 1 tablespoon vegetable oil
- 3 cloves garlic, minced
- 1 teaspoon grated ginger
- 4-5 baby bok choy, chopped
- 1 bell pepper, sliced
- 1 carrot, julienned
- 1/2 onion, thinly sliced
- Cooked rice or noodles, for serving

Instructions:

- In a small bowl, mix together the soy sauce and hoisin sauce. Add the cubed tofu to the bowl and toss to coat. Let it marinate for about 10-15 minutes.

- Heat the vegetable oil in a large skillet or wok over medium-high heat.

- Add the marinated tofu cubes to the skillet and cook for 4-5 minutes, or until golden brown on all sides. Remove the tofu from the skillet and set aside.

- In the same skillet, add the sesame oil, minced garlic, and grated ginger. Cook for 1-2 minutes, or until fragrant.

- Add the chopped bok choy, sliced bell pepper, julienned carrot, and thinly sliced onion to the skillet. Stir-fry for 3-4 minutes, or until the vegetables are tender-crisp.

- Return the cooked tofu to the skillet with the vegetables. Stir everything together and cook for another 1-2 minutes to heat through.

- Serve the tofu stir-fry hot over cooked rice or noodles.

This recipe is simple to prepare and doesn't require a lot of time or attention, making it suitable for individuals with ADHD. It's a flavorful and nutritious dish that's perfect for a quick and easy weeknight meal. Enjoy your tofu stir-fry with bok choy!

8. Turkey Chili with Beans

Ingredients:

- 1 tablespoon olive oil
- 1 onion, chopped
- 2 cloves garlic, minced
- 1 lb ground turkey
- 1 (15 oz) can diced tomatoes
- 1 (15 oz) can kidney beans, drained and rinsed
- 1 (15 oz) can black beans, drained and rinsed
- 1 cup corn kernels (fresh, frozen, or canned)
- 2 tablespoons chili powder
- 1 teaspoon ground cumin
- 1/2 teaspoon paprika
- Salt and pepper, to taste
- Optional toppings: shredded cheese, sliced green onions, sour cream, chopped cilantro

Instructions:

- Heat the olive oil in a large pot or Dutch oven over medium heat.

- Add the chopped onion and minced garlic to the pot. Cook for 3-4 minutes, or until softened.

- Add the ground turkey to the pot. Cook, breaking it up with a spoon, until browned and cooked through, about 5-6 minutes.

- Stir in the diced tomatoes, kidney beans, black beans, corn kernels, chili powder, ground cumin, paprika, salt, and pepper.

- Bring the chili to a simmer, then reduce the heat to low. Cover and let it simmer for about 20-25 minutes, stirring occasionally.

- Taste and adjust seasoning as needed.

- Serve the turkey chili hot, topped with your favorite toppings such as shredded cheese, sliced green onions, sour cream, or chopped cilantro.

This recipe is easy to prepare and doesn't require constant attention, making it suitable for individuals with ADHD. It's a hearty and comforting meal that's perfect for chilly evenings. Enjoy your turkey chili with beans!

9. Greek Salad with Feta and Olives

Ingredients:

- 2 large tomatoes, chopped
- 1 cucumber, diced
- 1 red onion, thinly sliced
- 1 bell pepper (any color), chopped
- 1/2 cup Kalamata olives, pitted
- 4 ounces feta cheese, crumbled
- 2 tablespoons extra virgin olive oil
- 1 tablespoon red wine vinegar
- 1 teaspoon dried oregano
- Salt and pepper, to taste
- Optional: chopped fresh parsley or basil for garnish

Instructions:

- In a large mixing bowl, combine the chopped tomatoes, diced cucumber, thinly sliced red onion, chopped bell pepper, and Kalamata olives.

- Add the crumbled feta cheese to the bowl.

- In a small bowl or jar, whisk together the extra virgin olive oil, red wine vinegar, dried oregano, salt, and pepper to make the dressing.

- Pour the dressing over the salad ingredients in the large mixing bowl.

- Toss everything together until well combined and evenly coated with the dressing.

- Taste and adjust seasoning as needed.

- Garnish with chopped fresh parsley or basil, if desired, before serving.

- Serve the Greek salad immediately, or chill it in the refrigerator for 30 minutes to allow the flavors to meld together before serving.

This recipe is quick and easy to prepare, making it suitable for individuals with ADHD. It's a refreshing and flavorful salad that's perfect as a side dish or light meal. Enjoy your Greek salad with feta and olives!

10. Lentil Soup with Spinach

Ingredients:
* 1 cup dried lentils (brown or green), rinsed and drained
* 1 onion, chopped
* 2 carrots, diced
* 2 celery stalks, diced
* 3 cloves garlic, minced
* 1 teaspoon ground cumin
* 1 teaspoon ground coriander
* 1/2 teaspoon smoked paprika
* 6 cups vegetable broth or water
* 2 cups fresh spinach leaves, chopped
* 2 tablespoons lemon juice
* Salt and pepper, to taste
* Optional toppings: chopped fresh parsley, grated Parmesan cheese, a dollop of Greek yogurt

Instructions:
* In a large pot or Dutch oven, heat a bit of oil over medium heat. Add the chopped onion, diced carrots, and diced celery. Cook, stirring occasionally, until the vegetables are softened, about 5-7 minutes.

* Add the minced garlic, ground cumin, ground coriander, and smoked paprika to the pot. Cook for another minute until fragrant.

* Add the rinsed lentils and vegetable broth or water to the pot. Bring the mixture to a boil, then reduce the heat to low and let it simmer, covered, for about 20-25 minutes, or until the lentils are tender.

* Once the lentils are cooked, stir in the chopped spinach leaves and lemon juice. Cook for an additional 1-2 minutes until the spinach is wilted.

* Taste the soup and adjust the seasoning with salt and pepper as needed. Ladle the lentil soup into bowls and serve hot.

* Optionally, garnish each bowl with chopped fresh parsley, grated Parmesan cheese, or a dollop of Greek yogurt before serving.

This recipe is straightforward and doesn't require too much attention to detail, making it suitable for individuals with ADHD. It's a nutritious and comforting soup that's perfect for a quick and easy meal. Enjoy your lentil soup with spinach!

11. Shrimp Stir-Fry with Snap Peas

Ingredients:

- 1 lb large shrimp, peeled and deveined
- Salt and pepper, to taste
- 2 tablespoons soy sauce
- 1 tablespoon oyster sauce
- 1 tablespoon sesame oil
- 2 tablespoons vegetable oil, divided
- 2 cloves garlic, minced
- 1 teaspoon grated ginger
-
- 2 cups snap peas, trimmed
- Cooked rice, for serving
- Optional Additions:
- Sliced bell peppers
- Sliced carrots
- Sliced mushrooms
- Sliced onions
- Cashews or peanuts for garnish

Instructions:

- Season the shrimp with salt and pepper to taste. In a small bowl, mix together the soy sauce, oyster sauce, and sesame oil. Add the shrimp to the bowl and toss to coat. Let it marinate for about 10-15 minutes.

- Heat 1 tablespoon of vegetable oil in a large skillet or wok over medium-high heat.

- Add the minced garlic and grated ginger to the skillet. Cook for about 1 minute until fragrant.

- Add the marinated shrimp to the skillet. Stir-fry for 2-3 minutes, or until the shrimp turn pink and are cooked through. Remove the shrimp from the skillet and set aside.

- In the same skillet, heat the remaining tablespoon of vegetable oil. Add the snap peas (and any other optional vegetables) to the skillet. Stir-fry for 2-3 minutes, or until the vegetables are tender-crisp.

- Return the cooked shrimp to the skillet with the snap peas. Stir everything together and cook for another minute to heat through.

- Serve the shrimp stir-fry hot over cooked rice. Optionally, garnish with cashews or peanuts before serving.

This recipe is quick and easy to prepare, making it suitable for individuals with ADHD. It's a delicious and nutritious meal that's perfect for a quick weeknight dinner. Enjoy your shrimp stir-fry with snap peas!

12. Stuffed Bell Peppers with Ground Turkey and Rice

Ingredients:

- 4 large bell peppers, any color
- 1 lb ground turkey
- 1 cup cooked rice (white or brown)
- 1 onion, diced
- 1 (15 oz) can diced tomatoes, drained
- 1 cup shredded cheese (such as cheddar or mozzarella)
- 1 teaspoon dried oregano
- 1 teaspoon dried basil
- 2 cloves garlic, minced
- Salt and pepper, to taste
- Optional: chopped fresh parsley or basil for garnish

Instructions:

- Preheat your oven to 375°F (190°C).

- Cut the tops off the bell peppers and remove the seeds and membranes from inside. Place the hollowed-out bell peppers in a baking dish, cut side up.

- In a skillet, cook the ground turkey over medium heat until browned and cooked through, breaking it up with a spoon as it cooks.

- Add the diced onion and minced garlic to the skillet with the cooked turkey. Cook for 2-3 minutes, or until the onion is softened.

- Stir in the cooked rice, diced tomatoes, dried oregano, dried basil, salt, and pepper. Cook for another 2-3 minutes, allowing the flavors to meld together.

- Remove the skillet from the heat and stir in half of the shredded cheese. Spoon the turkey and rice mixture into the hollowed-out bell peppers, packing it down gently.

- Cover the baking dish with aluminum foil and bake in the preheated oven for 30 minutes.

- Remove the foil from the baking dish and sprinkle the remaining shredded cheese over the tops of the stuffed bell peppers.

- Return the baking dish to the oven and bake, uncovered, for another 10-15 minutes, or until the cheese is melted and bubbly.

- Remove the stuffed bell peppers from the oven and let them cool for a few minutes before serving. Garnish with chopped fresh parsley or basil, if desired, before serving.

This recipe is easy to prepare and doesn't require constant attention, making it suitable for individuals with ADHD. It's a flavorful and satisfying meal that's perfect for a family dinner. Enjoy your stuffed bell peppers with ground turkey and rice!

13. Cauliflower Fried Rice

Ingredients:

- 1 head cauliflower
- 2 tablespoons vegetable oil or sesame oil
- 2 cloves garlic, minced
- 1 onion, diced
- 1 carrot, diced
- 1 cup frozen peas and carrots mix
- 2 eggs, lightly beaten
- 3 tablespoons soy sauce
- 1 teaspoon sesame oil
- Salt and pepper, to taste
- Optional: chopped green onions for garnish

Instructions:

- Cut the cauliflower into florets. Working in batches, pulse the cauliflower florets in a food processor until they resemble rice grains.

- Heat the vegetable oil or sesame oil in a large skillet or wok over medium-high heat.

- Add the minced garlic and diced onion to the skillet. Cook for 2-3 minutes, or until softened.

- Add the diced carrot and frozen peas and carrots mix to the skillet. Cook for another 3-4 minutes, or until the vegetables are tender.

- Push the vegetables to one side of the skillet and pour the beaten eggs into the empty side. Let them cook undisturbed for about 1 minute, then scramble them with a spatula until cooked through.

- Stir in the riced cauliflower to the skillet. Cook for 4-5 minutes, stirring occasionally, or until the cauliflower is tender.

- Drizzle the soy sauce and sesame oil over the cauliflower fried rice. Season with salt and pepper to taste. Stir everything together until well combined.

- Optionally, garnish with chopped green onions before serving.

This recipe is quick and easy to prepare, making it suitable for individuals with ADHD. It's a low-carb and nutritious alternative to traditional fried rice. Enjoy your cauliflower fried rice!

14. Baked Cod with Garlic Butter

Ingredients:
- 4 cod fillets (about 6 ounces each)
- Salt and pepper, to taste
- 4 tablespoons unsalted butter, melted
- 3 cloves garlic, minced
- 2 tablespoons chopped fresh parsley
- 1 tablespoon lemon juice
- Lemon wedges, for serving
- Optional: sliced cherry tomatoes for garnish

Instructions:

- Preheat your oven to 400°F (200°C). Line a baking dish with parchment paper or aluminum foil for easy cleanup.

- Pat the cod fillets dry with paper towels and place them in the prepared baking dish. Season both sides of the cod fillets with salt and pepper.

- In a small bowl, mix together the melted butter, minced garlic, chopped fresh parsley, and lemon juice.

- Pour the garlic butter mixture evenly over the cod fillets.

- If desired, scatter sliced cherry tomatoes around the cod fillets in the baking dish for extra flavor and color.

- Bake the cod in the preheated oven for 12-15 minutes, or until the fish is opaque and flakes easily with a fork.

- Remove the baked cod from the oven and let it rest for a few minutes.

- Serve the baked cod hot, with lemon wedges on the side for squeezing over the fish.

This recipe is simple to prepare and doesn't require constant attention, making it suitable for individuals with ADHD. It's a flavorful and healthy dish that's perfect for a quick and easy weeknight meal. Enjoy your baked cod with garlic butter!

15. Sweet Potato and Black Bean Tacos

Ingredients:

- 2 large sweet potatoes, peeled and diced
- 1 tablespoon olive oil
- 1 teaspoon ground cumin
- 1 teaspoon chili powder
- 1/2 teaspoon paprika
- Salt and pepper, to taste
- 1 (15 oz) can black beans, drained and rinsed
- 1 cup corn kernels (fresh, frozen, or canned)
- 1/2 cup diced red onion
- 1/4 cup chopped fresh cilantro
- 8 small corn or flour tortillas
- Optional toppings: sliced avocado, diced tomatoes, shredded cheese, sour cream, salsa

Instructions:

- Preheat your oven to 400Â°F (200Â°C).

- In a large bowl, toss the diced sweet potatoes with olive oil, ground cumin, chili powder, paprika, salt, and pepper until evenly coated.

- Spread the seasoned sweet potatoes out on a baking sheet lined with parchment paper or aluminum foil.

- Roast the sweet potatoes in the preheated oven for 20-25 minutes, or until tender and lightly browned, stirring halfway through.

- In a separate skillet, heat a bit of olive oil over medium heat. Add the drained and rinsed black beans, corn kernels, and diced red onion to the skillet. Cook for 5-6 minutes, stirring occasionally, until heated through and the onions are softened.

- Once the sweet potatoes are roasted, add them to the skillet with the black bean mixture. Stir in the chopped fresh cilantro and toss everything together.

- Warm the tortillas according to package instructions. Spoon the sweet potato and black bean mixture onto each tortilla.

- Top the tacos with your favorite toppings, such as sliced avocado, diced tomatoes, shredded cheese, sour cream, or salsa. Serve the sweet potato and black bean tacos immediately.

This recipe is easy to prepare and doesn't require constant attention, making it suitable for individuals with ADHD. It's a delicious and satisfying vegetarian meal option that's perfect for Taco Tuesday or any day of the week. Enjoy your sweet potato and black bean tacos!

16. Caprese Salad with Balsamic Glaze

Ingredients:
- 2 large ripe tomatoes, sliced
- 1 ball fresh mozzarella cheese, sliced
- Fresh basil leaves
- Balsamic glaze (store-bought or homemade)
- Extra virgin olive oil
- Salt and pepper, to taste

Instructions:

- Arrange the tomato slices and mozzarella cheese slices alternately on a serving platter or individual plates.

- Tuck fresh basil leaves between the tomato and mozzarella slices.

- Drizzle the caprese salad with balsamic glaze and extra virgin olive oil.

- Season with salt and pepper to taste.

- Optionally, garnish with additional fresh basil leaves for presentation.

This recipe is incredibly simple and requires minimal preparation, making it suitable for individuals with ADHD. It's a classic and refreshing salad that highlights the flavors of ripe tomatoes, creamy mozzarella, and fragrant basil, enhanced by the sweet tanginess of balsamic glaze. Enjoy your Caprese Salad with Balsamic Glaze!

17. Zucchini Noodles with Pesto

Ingredients:
- 4 medium zucchini
- 1/2 cup basil pesto (store-bought or homemade)
- Grated Parmesan cheese, for garnish (optional)
- Pine nuts or chopped walnuts, for garnish (optional)
- Fresh basil leaves, for garnish (optional)

Instructions:

- Wash the zucchini and trim off the ends. Use a spiralizer to turn the zucchini into noodles.

- Heat a bit of olive oil in a large skillet over medium heat. Add the zucchini noodles to the skillet and cook for 2-3 minutes, stirring occasionally, until just tender.

- Once the zucchini noodles are cooked, transfer them to a serving bowl.

- Add the basil pesto to the bowl with the zucchini noodles. Toss until the noodles are evenly coated with the pesto.

- Optionally, garnish the zucchini noodles with grated Parmesan cheese, pine nuts or chopped walnuts, and fresh basil leaves for extra flavor and presentation.

- Serve the zucchini noodles with pesto immediately as a light and nutritious meal or side dish.

This recipe is quick and easy to prepare, making it suitable for individuals with ADHD. It's a healthy and low-carb alternative to traditional pasta dishes, bursting with the flavors of fresh zucchini and fragrant basil pesto. Enjoy your Zucchini Noodles with Pesto!

18. Turkey Meatballs with Marinara Sauce

Ingredients:
- 1 lb ground turkey
- 1/2 cup breadcrumbs (you can use store-bought or homemade)
- 1/4 cup grated Parmesan cheese
- 1 egg, lightly beaten
- 2 cloves garlic, minced
- 1 teaspoon dried oregano
- 1 teaspoon dried basil
- Salt and pepper, to taste
- 2 cups marinara sauce (store-bought or homemade)

Instructions:
- Preheat your oven to 400Â°F (200Â°C). Line a baking sheet with parchment paper or aluminum foil for easy cleanup.

- In a large mixing bowl, combine the ground turkey, breadcrumbs, grated Parmesan cheese, lightly beaten egg, minced garlic, dried oregano, dried basil, salt, and pepper. Mix until well combined.

- Shape the turkey mixture into meatballs, about 1 to 1.5 inches in diameter, and place them on the prepared baking sheet.

- Bake the turkey meatballs in the preheated oven for 15-20 minutes, or until cooked through and lightly browned.

- While the meatballs are baking, heat the marinara sauce in a saucepan over medium heat until warmed through.

- Once the turkey meatballs are cooked, transfer them to the saucepan with the marinara sauce. Gently toss the meatballs in the sauce until they are evenly coated.

- Serve the turkey meatballs with marinara sauce hot, over cooked pasta, spaghetti squash, or zucchini noodles.

- Optionally, garnish with grated Parmesan cheese and chopped fresh basil before serving.

This recipe is easy to prepare and doesn't require constant attention, making it suitable for individuals with ADHD. It's a flavorful and nutritious meal that's perfect for a quick and easy dinner. Enjoy your turkey meatballs with marinara sauce!

19. Spinach and Feta Stuffed Chicken Breast

Ingredients:

- 4 boneless, skinless chicken breasts
- Salt and pepper, to taste
- 2 cups fresh spinach leaves
- 1/2 cup crumbled feta cheese
- 2 cloves garlic, minced
- 1 tablespoon olive oil
- Toothpicks or kitchen twine

Instructions:

- Preheat your oven to 375°F (190°C).

- Use a sharp knife to make a horizontal slit along the side of each chicken breast, creating a pocket for the stuffing. Be careful not to cut all the way through.

- Season the inside of each chicken breast with salt and pepper.

- In a skillet, heat the olive oil over medium heat. Add the minced garlic and sauté for 1-2 minutes, until fragrant.

- Add the fresh spinach leaves to the skillet and cook until wilted, about 2-3 minutes.

- Remove the skillet from the heat and stir in the crumbled feta cheese until well combined.

- Stuff each chicken breast with the spinach and feta mixture, dividing it evenly among the breasts. Secure the openings with toothpicks or tie with kitchen twine to keep the filling inside.

- Place the stuffed chicken breasts in a baking dish or on a baking sheet lined with parchment paper.

- Bake in the preheated oven for 25-30 minutes, or until the chicken is cooked through and no longer pink in the center.

- Remove the toothpicks or twine before serving. Optionally, garnish with chopped fresh parsley or a squeeze of lemon juice before serving.

This recipe is easy to prepare and doesn't require constant attention, making it suitable for individuals with ADHD. It's a flavorful and elegant dish that's perfect for a special dinner. Enjoy your spinach and feta stuffed chicken breast!

20. Chickpea Curry with Rice

Ingredients:
- 1 tablespoon vegetable oil
- 1 onion, chopped
- 3 cloves garlic, minced
- 1 tablespoon grated ginger
- 2 tablespoons curry powder
- 1 teaspoon ground cumin
- 1 teaspoon ground coriander
- 1/2 teaspoon turmeric powder
- 1/4 teaspoon cayenne pepper (adjust to taste)
- 1 (15 oz) can chickpeas, drained and rinsed
- 1 (14 oz) can diced tomatoes
- 1 cup coconut milk
- Salt and pepper, to taste
- Cooked rice, for serving
- Optional garnishes: chopped fresh cilantro, sliced green onions, lime wedges

Instructions:
- Heat the vegetable oil in a large skillet or pot over medium heat.

- Add the chopped onion to the skillet and cook for 3-4 minutes until softened.

- Add the minced garlic and grated ginger to the skillet. Cook for another 1-2 minutes until fragrant.

- Stir in the curry powder, ground cumin, ground coriander, turmeric powder, and cayenne pepper. Cook for 1 minute, stirring constantly.

- Add the drained and rinsed chickpeas, diced tomatoes (with their juices), and coconut milk to the skillet. Stir to combine.

- Bring the mixture to a simmer, then reduce the heat to low. Cover and let it simmer for 15-20 minutes, stirring occasionally, to allow the flavors to meld together and the sauce to thicken.

- Taste and season the chickpea curry with salt and pepper as needed. Serve the chickpea curry hot over cooked rice.

- Optionally, garnish with chopped fresh cilantro, sliced green onions, and lime wedges before serving.

This recipe is easy to prepare and doesn't require constant attention, making it suitable for individuals with ADHD. It's a flavorful and satisfying vegetarian meal that's perfect for a quick and easy weeknight dinner. Enjoy your chickpea curry with rice!

21. Greek Yogurt Parfait with Berries and Granola

Ingredients:
- 1 cup Greek yogurt (plain or flavored)
- 1/2 cup mixed berries (such as strawberries, blueberries, raspberries)
- 1/4 cup granola
- Optional: honey or maple syrup for drizzling

Instructions:

- Spoon a layer of Greek yogurt into the bottom of a serving glass or bowl.

- Add a layer of mixed berries on top of the yogurt.

- Sprinkle a layer of granola over the berries.

- Repeat the layers of yogurt, berries, and granola until the glass or bowl is filled or until you've used up all the ingredients.

- Optionally, drizzle honey or maple syrup over the top of the parfait for added sweetness.

- Serve the Greek yogurt parfait immediately, or cover and refrigerate until ready to eat.

This recipe is quick and easy to assemble, making it suitable for individuals with ADHD. It's a delicious and nutritious breakfast or snack option that's packed with protein, fiber, and vitamins from the Greek yogurt, berries, and granola. Enjoy your Greek Yogurt Parfait with Berries and Granola!

22. Roasted Vegetable Quesadillas

Ingredients:

- 2 large flour tortillas
- 1 cup shredded cheese (such as cheddar, Monterey Jack, or a Mexican blend)
- 1 bell pepper, sliced
- 1 onion, sliced
- 1 zucchini, sliced
- 1 cup sliced mushrooms
- 2 tablespoons olive oil
- Salt and pepper, to taste
- Optional toppings: salsa, guacamole, sour cream, chopped cilantro

Instructions:

- Preheat your oven to 400°F (200°C).

- Place the sliced bell pepper, onion, zucchini, and mushrooms on a baking sheet. Drizzle with olive oil and season with salt and pepper. Toss to coat the vegetables evenly.

- Roast the vegetables in the preheated oven for 15-20 minutes, or until they are tender and lightly browned, stirring halfway through.

- Heat a large skillet over medium heat. Place one flour tortilla in the skillet. Sprinkle half of the shredded cheese over one half of the tortilla.

- Arrange a portion of the roasted vegetables over the cheese. Sprinkle the remaining shredded cheese over the vegetables. Fold the other half of the tortilla over the filling to form a half-moon shape.

- Cook the quesadilla for 2-3 minutes on each side, or until the tortilla is golden brown and the cheese is melted. Repeat the process with the remaining tortilla and filling ingredients.

- Once both quesadillas are cooked, transfer them to a cutting board and let them cool for a minute.

- Use a sharp knife to cut each quesadilla into wedges. Serve the roasted vegetable quesadillas hot, with your favorite toppings such as salsa, guacamole, sour cream, or chopped cilantro.

This recipe is easy to prepare and doesn't require constant attention, making it suitable for individuals with ADHD. It's a flavorful and satisfying meal that's perfect for a quick and easy lunch or dinner. Enjoy your roasted vegetable quesadillas!

23. Eggplant Parmesan

Ingredients:
- 2 large eggplants, sliced into 1/2-inch rounds
- Salt
- 2 cups breadcrumbs (you can use store-bought or homemade)
- 1 cup grated Parmesan cheese
- 2 eggs, beaten
- 2 cups marinara sauce (store-bought or homemade)
- 2 cups shredded mozzarella cheese
- Fresh basil leaves, for garnish (optional)

Instructions:
- Preheat your oven to 375°F (190°C). Line a baking sheet with parchment paper.

- Place the sliced eggplant rounds in a single layer on the prepared baking sheet. Sprinkle both sides of the eggplant slices with salt and let them sit for about 10-15 minutes. This helps draw out excess moisture from the eggplant.

- After 10-15 minutes, pat the eggplant slices dry with paper towels to remove the excess moisture. In a shallow dish, mix together the breadcrumbs and grated Parmesan cheese.

- Dip each eggplant slice into the beaten eggs, then dredge it in the breadcrumb mixture, coating both sides evenly. Place the breaded eggplant slices back onto the baking sheet.

- Bake the breaded eggplant slices in the preheated oven for 20-25 minutes, or until golden brown and tender, flipping halfway through.

- Remove the baked eggplant slices from the oven and increase the oven temperature to 400°F (200°C). In a baking dish, spread a thin layer of marinara sauce on the bottom.

- Arrange half of the baked eggplant slices in the baking dish in a single layer. Spoon marinara sauce over each eggplant slice, then sprinkle shredded mozzarella cheese on top.

- Repeat with the remaining eggplant slices, marinara sauce, and shredded mozzarella cheese.

- Bake the assembled Eggplant Parmesan in the preheated oven for 20-25 minutes, or until the cheese is melted and bubbly. Remove from the oven and let it cool for a few minutes before serving. Garnish with fresh basil leaves, if desired, before serving.

This recipe is easy to prepare and doesn't require constant attention, making it suitable for individuals with ADHD. It's a delicious and comforting dish that's perfect for a cozy dinner. Enjoy your Eggplant Parmesan!

24. Butternut Squash Soup

Ingredients:

- 1 large butternut squash, peeled, seeded, and cubed
- 1 onion, chopped
- 2 cloves garlic, minced
- 2 carrots, chopped
- 2 stalks celery, chopped
- 4 cups vegetable broth or chicken broth
- 1 teaspoon dried thyme
- 1/2 teaspoon ground cinnamon
- Salt and pepper, to taste
- 2 tablespoons olive oil
- Optional garnishes: toasted pumpkin seeds, a dollop of sour cream, chopped fresh parsley

Instructions:

- In a large pot or Dutch oven, heat the olive oil over medium heat.

- Add the chopped onion, minced garlic, chopped carrots, and chopped celery to the pot. Cook, stirring occasionally, for about 5 minutes until the vegetables are softened.

- Add the cubed butternut squash to the pot, along with the dried thyme and ground cinnamon. Season with salt and pepper to taste. Cook for another 2-3 minutes, stirring occasionally.

- Pour the vegetable broth or chicken broth into the pot, making sure the butternut squash and vegetables are submerged.

- Bring the soup to a boil, then reduce the heat to low. Cover and let it simmer for about 20-25 minutes, or until the butternut squash is tender and easily pierced with a fork.

- Once the butternut squash is cooked, use an immersion blender to puree the soup until smooth. Alternatively, you can carefully transfer the soup in batches to a blender and blend until smooth, then return it to the pot. Taste and adjust seasoning with salt and pepper if needed.

- If the soup is too thick, you can add more broth or water to reach your desired consistency. Serve the butternut squash soup hot, garnished with toasted pumpkin seeds, a dollop of sour cream, and chopped fresh parsley, if desired.

This recipe is easy to prepare and doesn't require constant attention, making it suitable for individuals with ADHD. It's a comforting and nutritious soup that's perfect for chilly days. Enjoy your Butternut Squash Soup!

25. Lemon Herb Roast Chicken

Ingredients:
- 1 whole chicken (about 3-4 pounds)
- Salt and pepper, to taste
- 1 lemon, halved
- 4 cloves garlic, minced
- 2 tablespoons chopped fresh herbs (such as rosemary, thyme, and parsley)
- 2 tablespoons olive oil

Instructions:
- Preheat your oven to 425°F (220°C).

- Remove any giblets from the cavity of the chicken and pat it dry with paper towels.

- Season the inside and outside of the chicken generously with salt and pepper.

- Squeeze the juice of one lemon half over the chicken, then place the lemon halves inside the cavity of the chicken.

- In a small bowl, mix together the minced garlic, chopped fresh herbs, and olive oil to make a herb paste.

- Rub the herb paste all over the outside of the chicken, ensuring it's evenly coated.

- Place the chicken breast-side up in a roasting pan or baking dish.

- Roast the chicken in the preheated oven for about 1 hour to 1 hour 15 minutes, or until the internal temperature reaches 165°F (75°C) when measured with a meat thermometer inserted into the thickest part of the thigh.

- Once the chicken is cooked through and golden brown, remove it from the oven and let it rest for about 10-15 minutes before carving.

- Carve the roasted chicken into serving portions and serve hot.

- Optionally, you can squeeze the remaining lemon half over the carved chicken for extra flavor.

This recipe is easy to prepare and doesn't require constant attention, making it suitable for individuals with ADHD. It's a delicious and comforting meal that's perfect for a family dinner or special occasion. Enjoy your Lemon Herb Roast Chicken!

26. Asian Slaw with Peanut Dressing

Ingredients:

- 4 cups shredded cabbage (green or purple)
- 1 cup shredded carrots
- 1 bell pepper, thinly sliced
- 1/2 cup chopped cilantro
- 1/4 cup chopped green onions
- 1/4 cup chopped peanuts (for garnish, optional)
- Peanut Dressing:
- 1/4 cup creamy peanut butter
- 2 tablespoons soy sauce
- 2 tablespoons rice vinegar
- 1 tablespoon honey or maple syrup
- 1 tablespoon sesame oil
- 1 clove garlic, minced
- 1 teaspoon grated ginger
- 2-3 tablespoons water (to thin the dressing, if needed)

Instructions:

- In a large bowl, combine the shredded cabbage, shredded carrots, sliced bell pepper, chopped cilantro, and chopped green onions. Toss to mix well.

- In a separate small bowl, whisk together the creamy peanut butter, soy sauce, rice vinegar, honey or maple syrup, sesame oil, minced garlic, and grated ginger until smooth. If the dressing is too thick, you can thin it out with 2-3 tablespoons of water until you reach your desired consistency.

- Pour the peanut dressing over the cabbage mixture in the large bowl.

- Toss the slaw with the peanut dressing until the vegetables are evenly coated.

- Optionally, garnish the Asian slaw with chopped peanuts for extra crunch and flavor.

- Serve the Asian Slaw with Peanut Dressing immediately as a side dish or as a light and refreshing salad.

This recipe is easy to prepare and doesn't require constant attention, making it suitable for individuals with ADHD. It's a flavorful and nutritious dish that's perfect for a quick and easy lunch or dinner. Enjoy your Asian Slaw with Peanut Dressing!

27. Baked Teriyaki Salmon

Ingredients:
- 4 salmon fillets (about 6 ounces each)
- Salt and pepper, to taste
- 1/2 cup teriyaki sauce (store-bought or homemade)
- 2 tablespoons honey or brown sugar
- 2 cloves garlic, minced
- 1 tablespoon grated ginger
- 1 tablespoon sesame seeds (for garnish, optional)
- Sliced green onions (for garnish, optional)

Instructions:

- Preheat your oven to 400Â°F (200Â°C). Line a baking sheet with parchment paper or aluminum foil for easy cleanup.

- Place the salmon fillets on the prepared baking sheet. Season both sides of the salmon with salt and pepper to taste.

- In a small bowl, mix together the teriyaki sauce, honey or brown sugar, minced garlic, and grated ginger.

- Pour the teriyaki sauce mixture over the salmon fillets, ensuring they are evenly coated.

- Bake the salmon in the preheated oven for 12-15 minutes, or until the salmon is cooked through and flakes easily with a fork.

- While the salmon is baking, you can baste it with the teriyaki sauce from the baking sheet a couple of times during cooking, if desired.

- Once the salmon is cooked, remove it from the oven and let it rest for a few minutes.

- Optionally, garnish the baked teriyaki salmon with sesame seeds and sliced green onions before serving.

- Serve the baked teriyaki salmon hot, with your favorite sides such as steamed rice and vegetables.

This recipe is easy to prepare and doesn't require constant attention, making it suitable for individuals with ADHD. It's a flavorful and healthy dish that's perfect for a quick and easy weeknight dinner. Enjoy your Baked Teriyaki Salmon!

28. Quinoa Stuffed Peppers

Ingredients:

- 4 large bell peppers (any color)
- 1 cup quinoa, rinsed
- 2 cups vegetable broth or water
- 1 tablespoon olive oil
- 1 onion, diced
- 2 cloves garlic, minced
- 1 zucchini, diced
- 1 cup diced tomatoes (fresh or canned)
- 1 teaspoon dried oregano
- 1 teaspoon dried basil
- Salt and pepper, to taste
- 1 carrot, diced
- 1 cup shredded cheese (such as cheddar or mozzarella), divided
- Optional garnish: chopped fresh parsley or basil

Instructions:

- Preheat your oven to 375°F (190°C). Grease a baking dish large enough to hold the bell peppers.

- Cut the tops off the bell peppers and remove the seeds and membranes from inside. Place the hollowed-out bell peppers in the prepared baking dish, cut side up.

- In a medium saucepan, bring the vegetable broth or water to a boil. Add the rinsed quinoa, reduce the heat to low, cover, and simmer for about 15 minutes, or until the quinoa is cooked and the liquid is absorbed.

- In a large skillet, heat the olive oil over medium heat. Add the diced onion and minced garlic to the skillet. Cook for 2-3 minutes, or until softened.

- Add the diced zucchini and carrot to the skillet. Cook for another 3-4 minutes, or until the vegetables are tender.

- Stir in the diced tomatoes, dried oregano, dried basil, salt, and pepper. Cook for another 2-3 minutes, allowing the flavors to meld together. Remove the skillet from the heat and stir in the cooked quinoa and half of the shredded cheese.

- Spoon the quinoa mixture into the hollowed-out bell peppers, packing it down gently. Sprinkle the remaining shredded cheese over the tops of the stuffed bell peppers.

- Cover the baking dish with aluminum foil and bake in the preheated oven for 25-30 minutes. Remove the foil from the baking dish and bake, uncovered, for another 10-15 minutes, or until the peppers are tender and the cheese is melted and bubbly.

- Remove the stuffed peppers from the oven and let them cool for a few minutes before serving. Optionally, garnish with chopped fresh parsley or basil before serving.

29. Stir-Fried Tofu with Vegetables

Ingredients:

- 1 block (14 oz) firm tofu, drained and pressed
- 2 tablespoons soy sauce
- 1 tablespoon rice vinegar
- 1 tablespoon honey or maple syrup
- 1 teaspoon sesame oil
- 1 tablespoon cornstarch
- 2 tablespoons vegetable oil, divided
- 2 cloves garlic, minced
- 1 tablespoon grated ginger
- 1 bell pepper, thinly sliced
- 1 cup broccoli florets
- 1 carrot, thinly sliced
- 1 cup snap peas or snow peas
- Salt and pepper, to taste
- Cooked rice or noodles, for serving
- Optional garnishes: chopped green onions, sesame seeds

Instructions:

- Cut the pressed tofu into cubes or rectangles.

- In a small bowl, whisk together the soy sauce, rice vinegar, honey or maple syrup, sesame oil, and cornstarch until well combined. Set aside.

- Heat 1 tablespoon of vegetable oil in a large skillet or wok over medium-high heat.

- Add the cubed tofu to the skillet and cook for 5-7 minutes, or until golden brown and crispy on all sides, stirring occasionally. Remove the tofu from the skillet and set it aside.

- In the same skillet, heat the remaining tablespoon of vegetable oil over medium-high heat. Add the minced garlic and grated ginger to the skillet and cook for 1-2 minutes, until fragrant.

- Add the sliced bell pepper, broccoli florets, sliced carrot, and snap peas or snow peas to the skillet. Stir-fry for 5-7 minutes, or until the vegetables are tender-crisp.

- Return the cooked tofu to the skillet with the stir-fried vegetables.

- Pour the soy sauce mixture over the tofu and vegetables in the skillet. Stir-fry for another 2-3 minutes, or until the sauce has thickened and coats the tofu and vegetables evenly.

- Season with salt and pepper to taste. Serve the stir-fried tofu with vegetables hot, over cooked rice or noodles. Optionally, garnish with chopped green onions and sesame seeds before serving.

This recipe is easy to prepare and doesn't require constant attention, making it suitable for individuals with ADHD. It's a flavorful and satisfying vegetarian dish that's perfect for a quick and easy weeknight dinner. Enjoy your Stir-Fried Tofu with Vegetables!

30. Turkey and Vegetable Skewers

Ingredients:
- 1 lb turkey breast, cut into 1-inch cubes
- 2 bell peppers (any color), cut into chunks
- 1 red onion, cut into chunks
- 1 zucchini, sliced into rounds
- 8-10 cherry tomatoes
- Wooden or metal skewers
- Salt and pepper, to taste
- Olive oil, for brushing
- Optional marinade: your favorite store-bought marinade or a simple mixture of olive oil, lemon juice, minced garlic, dried herbs, salt, and pepper

Instructions:
- If using wooden skewers, soak them in water for at least 30 minutes to prevent burning.
- Preheat your grill or grill pan to medium-high heat.
- Thread the turkey cubes and prepared vegetables onto the skewers, alternating between the turkey and vegetables.
- Season the skewers with salt and pepper to taste.
- Optionally, you can marinate the skewers in your favorite marinade for about 30 minutes to enhance flavor. If marinating, make sure to drain excess marinade before grilling.
- Brush the grill grates or grill pan with olive oil to prevent sticking.
- Place the skewers on the preheated grill or grill pan. Cook for 8-10 minutes, turning occasionally, until the turkey is cooked through and the vegetables are tender and slightly charred.
- Once the turkey and vegetables are cooked, remove the skewers from the grill and let them rest for a few minutes before serving.
- Serve the turkey and vegetable skewers hot, either as is or with your favorite side dishes such as rice, salad, or grilled bread.
- Optionally, you can drizzle the skewers with a little extra olive oil or squeeze some lemon juice over the top before serving for added flavor.

This recipe is easy to prepare and doesn't require constant attention, making it suitable for individuals with ADHD. It's a delicious and healthy dish that's perfect for a summer barbecue or a quick and easy weeknight meal. Enjoy your Turkey and Vegetable Skewers!

31. Mediterranean Chickpea Salad

Ingredients:

- 2 cans (15 oz each) chickpeas, drained and rinsed
- 1 cucumber, diced
- 1 pint cherry tomatoes, halved
- 1/2 red onion, thinly sliced
- 1/2 cup Kalamata olives, pitted and halved
- 1/2 cup crumbled feta cheese
- 1/4 cup chopped fresh parsley
- 1/4 cup chopped fresh basil
- 2 tablespoons extra virgin olive oil
- 2 tablespoons red wine vinegar
- Salt and pepper, to taste
- Optional: lemon wedges, for serving

Instructions:

- In a large mixing bowl, combine the chickpeas, diced cucumber, halved cherry tomatoes, sliced red onion, halved Kalamata olives, crumbled feta cheese, chopped fresh parsley, and chopped fresh basil.

- Drizzle the extra virgin olive oil and red wine vinegar over the salad ingredients.

- Season with salt and pepper to taste.

- Toss the salad until all the ingredients are evenly coated with the dressing.

- Taste and adjust seasoning if needed.

- Optionally, let the salad marinate in the refrigerator for about 30 minutes to allow the flavors to meld together.

- Serve the Mediterranean Chickpea Salad chilled or at room temperature.

- Optionally, garnish with lemon wedges for squeezing over the salad before serving.

This recipe is easy to prepare and doesn't require constant attention, making it suitable for individuals with ADHD. It's a flavorful and nutritious salad that's perfect for a light lunch or side dish. Enjoy your Mediterranean Chickpea Salad!

32. Ratatouille

Ingredients:

- 1 eggplant, diced
- 2 zucchini, diced
- 1 yellow bell pepper, diced
- 1 red bell pepper, diced
- 1 onion, diced
- 3 cloves garlic, minced
- 2 cups diced tomatoes (fresh or canned)
- 2 tablespoons tomato paste
- 2 tablespoons olive oil
- 1 teaspoon dried thyme
- 1 teaspoon dried oregano
- Salt and pepper, to taste
- Optional: chopped fresh basil or parsley for garnish

Instructions:

- Heat the olive oil in a large skillet or pot over medium heat. Add the diced onion to the skillet and cook for 2-3 minutes until softened. Add the minced garlic to the skillet and cook for another 1-2 minutes until fragrant.

- Add the diced eggplant, diced zucchini, diced bell peppers, dried thyme, and dried oregano to the skillet. Season with salt and pepper to taste. Cook, stirring occasionally, for about 5-7 minutes until the vegetables start to soften.

- Stir in the diced tomatoes and tomato paste. Bring the mixture to a simmer.

- Reduce the heat to low, cover, and let the ratatouille simmer for about 20-25 minutes, stirring occasionally, until the vegetables are tender and the flavors have melded together.

- Taste and adjust seasoning with salt and pepper if needed. Once the ratatouille is cooked, remove it from the heat and let it cool slightly before serving.

- Optionally, garnish the ratatouille with chopped fresh basil or parsley before serving. Serve the ratatouille hot as a main dish, side dish, or over cooked pasta, rice, or crusty bread.

This recipe is easy to prepare and doesn't require constant attention, making it suitable for individuals with ADHD. It's a delicious and comforting dish that's perfect for a cozy dinner. Enjoy your Ratatouille!

33. Cauliflower Pizza Crust with Toppings

Ingredients:
- 1 medium head cauliflower, cut into florets
- 1/4 cup grated Parmesan cheese
- 1/4 cup shredded mozzarella cheese
- 1/2 teaspoon dried oregano
- 1/2 teaspoon dried basil
- 1/4 teaspoon garlic powder
- 1/4 teaspoon salt
- 1 large egg, beaten
- Pizza toppings of your choice (such as tomato sauce, shredded cheese, vegetables, meats)

Instructions:
- Preheat your oven to 400°F (200°C). Line a baking sheet with parchment paper.

- Place the cauliflower florets in a food processor and pulse until they resemble fine crumbs, resembling the texture of rice.

- Transfer the cauliflower crumbs to a microwave-safe bowl and microwave on high for 4-5 minutes until softened.

- Let the cauliflower cool for a few minutes, then transfer it to a clean kitchen towel or cheesecloth. Squeeze out as much moisture as possible from the cauliflower.

- In a large mixing bowl, combine the drained cauliflower with the grated Parmesan cheese, shredded mozzarella cheese, dried oregano, dried basil, garlic powder, salt, and beaten egg. Mix until well combined.

- Place the cauliflower mixture onto the prepared baking sheet and use your hands to shape it into a thin, round crust, about 1/4-inch thick.

- Bake the cauliflower crust in the preheated oven for 20-25 minutes, or until golden brown and firm to the touch. Once the crust is baked, remove it from the oven and let it cool for a few minutes.

Toppings:
- Spread tomato sauce or your favorite pizza sauce over the baked cauliflower crust. Sprinkle shredded cheese over the sauce, then add your desired toppings such as vegetables, meats, or additional cheese.

- Return the topped pizza to the oven and bake for another 10-15 minutes, or until the cheese is melted and bubbly.

- Once the pizza is cooked to your liking, remove it from the oven and let it cool for a few minutes before slicing. Slice the cauliflower pizza into wedges and serve hot.

34. Thai Green Curry with Chicken

Ingredients:

- 1 lb boneless, skinless chicken breast or thighs, cut into bite-sized pieces
- 1 tablespoon vegetable oil
- 3 tablespoons Thai green curry paste (store-bought or homemade)
- 1 can (13.5 oz) coconut milk
- 1 cup chicken broth
- 2 tablespoons fish sauce
- 1 tablespoon brown sugar
- 1 bell pepper, sliced
- 1 zucchini, sliced
- 1 cup sliced mushrooms
- 1 cup baby spinach or chopped kale
- 1 tablespoon lime juice
- Fresh cilantro, for garnish (optional)
- Cooked rice, for serving

Instructions:

- Heat the vegetable oil in a large skillet or wok over medium-high heat.

- Add the Thai green curry paste to the skillet and cook for 1-2 minutes, stirring constantly, until fragrant.

- Add the chicken pieces to the skillet and cook until browned on all sides, about 5-7 minutes.

- Pour in the coconut milk and chicken broth, stirring to combine. Stir in the fish sauce and brown sugar, then bring the mixture to a simmer.

- Add the sliced bell pepper, zucchini, and mushrooms to the skillet. Simmer for 5-7 minutes, or until the vegetables are tender and the chicken is cooked through.

- Stir in the baby spinach or chopped kale until wilted. Remove the skillet from the heat and stir in the lime juice.

- Taste and adjust the seasoning with more fish sauce or lime juice if needed. Serve the Thai Green Curry with Chicken hot, over cooked rice. Optionally, garnish with fresh cilantro before serving.

This recipe is easy to prepare and doesn't require constant attention, making it suitable for individuals with ADHD. It's a flavorful and aromatic dish that's perfect for a quick and easy weeknight dinner. Enjoy your Thai Green Curry with Chicken!

35. Sautéed Shrimp with Garlic and Lemon

Ingredients:

- 1 lb large shrimp, peeled and deveined
- 2 tablespoons olive oil
- 4 cloves garlic, minced
- 1/2 teaspoon red pepper flakes (optional, for a bit of heat)
- Salt and pepper, to taste
- Juice of 1 lemon
- 2 tablespoons chopped fresh parsley
- Lemon wedges, for serving

Instructions:

- Heat the olive oil in a large skillet over medium-high heat.

- Add the minced garlic and red pepper flakes (if using) to the skillet. SautÃ© for 1-2 minutes, or until the garlic is fragrant and lightly golden.

- Add the shrimp to the skillet in a single layer. Season with salt and pepper to taste.

- Cook the shrimp for about 2-3 minutes on each side, or until they turn pink and opaque.

- Squeeze the juice of one lemon over the shrimp and give everything a quick stir to coat the shrimp in the lemon juice.

- Remove the skillet from the heat and sprinkle the chopped fresh parsley over the shrimp.

- Serve the sautÃ©ed shrimp hot, with lemon wedges on the side for extra flavor.

This recipe is quick and easy to prepare, making it suitable for individuals with ADHD. It's a delicious and healthy dish that's perfect for a light dinner or as a topping for salads or pasta. Enjoy your SautÃ©ed Shrimp with Garlic and Lemon!

36. Baked Falafel with Tahini Sauce

Ingredients:
- 1 can (15 oz) chickpeas, drained and rinsed
- 1/4 cup chopped onion
- 2 cloves garlic, minced
- 1/4 cup chopped fresh parsley
- 1/4 cup chopped fresh cilantro
- 1 teaspoon ground cumin
- 1 teaspoon ground coriander
- 1/2 teaspoon baking powder
- 1/4 cup all-purpose flour or chickpea flour
- Salt and pepper, to taste
- 2 tablespoons olive oil

Instructions:
- Preheat your oven to 375°F (190°C). Line a baking sheet with parchment paper or lightly grease it.

- In a food processor, combine the chickpeas, chopped onion, minced garlic, parsley, cilantro, ground cumin, ground coriander, baking powder, flour, salt, and pepper. Pulse until the mixture is well combined but still slightly coarse.

- Scoop out small portions of the mixture and shape them into balls or patties, about 1-2 inches in diameter. Place them on the prepared baking sheet.

- Brush the tops of the falafel balls or patties with olive oil. Bake in the preheated oven for 20-25 minutes, turning them halfway through, until they are golden brown and crispy on the outside.

Tahini Sauce
Ingredients:
- 1/4 cup tahini
- 2 tablespoons lemon juice
- 1 clove garlic, minced
- 2-3 tablespoons water (to thin the sauce)
- Salt, to taste

Instructions:
- In a small bowl, whisk together the tahini, lemon juice, minced garlic, and a pinch of salt.

- Gradually add water, one tablespoon at a time, until the sauce reaches your desired consistency. Taste and adjust seasoning if needed.

Serve the baked falafel warm with the tahini sauce on the side for dipping. Optionally, serve with pita bread, chopped vegetables (like cucumber, tomatoes, and red onion), and a sprinkle of fresh herbs for a complete meal.

This recipe is easy to prepare and doesn't require constant attention, making it suitable for individuals with ADHD. It's a delicious and healthy dish that's perfect for lunch or dinner. Enjoy your Baked Falafel with Tahini Sauce!

37. Coconut Curry Lentil Soup

Ingredients:

- 1 tablespoon olive oil
- 1 onion, diced
- 3 cloves garlic, minced
- 1 tablespoon ginger, grated
- 1-2 tablespoons red curry paste (to taste)
- 1 cup red lentils, rinsed
- 1 can (14 oz) coconut milk
- 4 cups vegetable broth
- 1 can (14 oz) diced tomatoes
- 2 cups chopped spinach or kale
- 1 tablespoon lime juice
- Salt and pepper, to taste
- Fresh cilantro, for garnish (optional)

Instructions:

- Heat the olive oil in a large pot over medium heat.

- Add the diced onion and cook for about 3-4 minutes until it starts to soften.

- Add the minced garlic and grated ginger to the pot and cook for another 1-2 minutes until fragrant.

- Stir in the red curry paste and cook for 1-2 minutes, allowing the flavors to blend.

- Add the rinsed red lentils, coconut milk, vegetable broth, and diced tomatoes (with their juices) to the pot. Stir to combine.

- Bring the mixture to a boil, then reduce the heat to low and simmer for about 20-25 minutes, or until the lentils are tender.

- Stir in the chopped spinach or kale and cook for another 2-3 minutes until wilted.

- Add the lime juice and season with salt and pepper to taste. Remove the pot from the heat and let the soup cool slightly before serving.

- Optionally, garnish with fresh cilantro before serving. Serve the Coconut Curry Lentil Soup hot, with crusty bread or rice if desired.

This recipe is easy to prepare and doesn't require constant attention, making it suitable for individuals with ADHD. It's a flavorful and hearty soup that's perfect for a comforting and nutritious meal. Enjoy your Coconut Curry Lentil Soup!

38. Avocado Chicken Salad

Ingredients:
- 2 cups cooked chicken breast, shredded or diced
- 1 large avocado, diced
- 1/4 cup red onion, finely chopped
- 1/2 cup cherry tomatoes, halved
- 1/4 cup cilantro, chopped
- Juice of 1 lime
- 2 tablespoons Greek yogurt or mayonnaise
- Salt and pepper, to taste

Instructions:

- In a large mixing bowl, combine the shredded or diced chicken, diced avocado, chopped red onion, halved cherry tomatoes, and chopped cilantro.

- In a small bowl, whisk together the lime juice and Greek yogurt or mayonnaise until smooth.

- Pour the lime dressing over the chicken and avocado mixture.

- Gently toss the salad until all the ingredients are well coated with the dressing.

- Season with salt and pepper to taste.

- Serve the Avocado Chicken Salad immediately, either on its own, in a sandwich, wrap, or on a bed of greens.

This recipe is easy to prepare and doesn't require constant attention, making it suitable for individuals with ADHD. It's a nutritious and satisfying dish that's perfect for lunch or a light dinner. Enjoy your Avocado Chicken Salad!

39. Turkey and Spinach Stuffed Mushrooms

Ingredients:

- 12 large mushrooms (such as cremini or button), stems removed and finely chopped
- 1 tablespoon olive oil
- 1/2 lb ground turkey
- 2 cloves garlic, minced
- 1/2 cup finely chopped onion
- 2 cups fresh spinach, chopped
- 1/4 cup grated Parmesan cheese
- 1/4 cup breadcrumbs
- 1/2 teaspoon dried oregano
- Salt and pepper, to taste
- 1/4 cup shredded mozzarella cheese (optional)

Instructions:

- Preheat your oven to 375°F (190°C). Line a baking sheet with parchment paper or lightly grease it.

- Heat the olive oil in a skillet over medium heat. Add the chopped mushroom stems, minced garlic, and chopped onion. Cook for about 5 minutes, until the vegetables are soft and fragrant.

- Add the ground turkey to the skillet and cook until browned, breaking it up with a spoon as it cooks, about 7-8 minutes.

- Stir in the chopped spinach and cook for another 2-3 minutes until wilted.

- Remove the skillet from heat and stir in the grated Parmesan cheese, breadcrumbs, dried oregano, salt, and pepper. Mix until well combined.

- Spoon the turkey and spinach mixture into the mushroom caps, pressing down lightly to fill them.

- Place the stuffed mushrooms on the prepared baking sheet. Optionally, sprinkle shredded mozzarella cheese on top of each stuffed mushroom.

- Bake in the preheated oven for 20-25 minutes, until the mushrooms are tender and the tops are golden brown. Remove from the oven and let cool slightly before serving.

- Serve the Turkey and Spinach Stuffed Mushrooms as an appetizer, side dish, or light main course.

This recipe is easy to prepare and doesn't require constant attention, making it suitable for individuals with ADHD. It's a delicious and nutritious dish that's perfect for any meal. Enjoy your Turkey and Spinach Stuffed Mushrooms!

40. Teriyaki Tofu Bowl with Vegetables

41. Grilled Veggie Panini

Ingredients:
- 1 medium zucchini, sliced
- 1 medium yellow squash, sliced
- 1 red bell pepper, sliced
- 1 small red onion, sliced
- 2 tablespoons olive oil
- Salt and pepper to taste
- 4 slices of your favorite bread (sourdough or whole wheat work well)
- 4 slices provolone cheese (or cheese of your choice)
- Pesto sauce (optional)
- Butter or olive oil for grilling

Instructions:
- Preheat your grill or grill pan to medium-high heat.

- In a bowl, toss the sliced zucchini, yellow squash, red bell pepper, and red onion with olive oil, salt, and pepper until evenly coated.

- Grill the vegetables for 3-4 minutes per side, or until they are tender and have grill marks.

- While the veggies are grilling, assemble your sandwiches. Spread pesto sauce (if using) on one side of each slice of bread.

- Place a slice of cheese on each slice of bread, then add a generous portion of grilled vegetables on top of the cheese.

- Close the sandwiches with the remaining slices of bread.

- Brush the outsides of the sandwiches with butter or olive oil.

- Place the sandwiches on the grill or grill pan and cook for 3-4 minutes per side, or until the bread is toasted and the cheese is melted.

- Remove from the grill, let cool for a minute, then slice diagonally and serve hot.

Enjoy your delicious Grilled Veggie Panini! And remember, for ADHD management, finding routines, breaking tasks into smaller steps, and using tools like planners or reminders can be helpful.

42. Lemon Garlic Shrimp Pasta

Ingredients:
- 8 oz (225g) pasta (linguine or spaghetti works well)
- 1 lb (450g) large shrimp, peeled and deveined
- 4 cloves garlic, minced
- Zest of 1 lemon
- Juice of 1 lemon
- 3 tablespoons olive oil
- Salt and pepper to taste
- Crushed red pepper flakes (optional)
- 2 tablespoons chopped fresh parsley
- Grated Parmesan cheese for serving

Instructions:

- Cook the pasta according to package instructions until al dente. Drain and set aside.

- While the pasta is cooking, heat 2 tablespoons of olive oil in a large skillet over medium heat.

- Add the minced garlic to the skillet and sauté for 1-2 minutes, until fragrant.

- Add the shrimp to the skillet and season with salt, pepper, and crushed red pepper flakes if using. Cook the shrimp for 2-3 minutes on each side, or until they are pink and cooked through.

- Once the shrimp are cooked, remove them from the skillet and set aside.

- In the same skillet, add the cooked pasta, lemon zest, lemon juice, remaining 1 tablespoon of olive oil, and chopped parsley. Toss everything together until well combined and heated through.

- Taste and adjust seasoning if necessary.

- Serve the lemon garlic shrimp pasta hot, topped with the cooked shrimp and grated Parmesan cheese.

This Lemon Garlic Shrimp Pasta is bursting with flavor and makes for a satisfying meal. Enjoy! And remember, maintaining a balanced lifestyle with regular routines and healthy habits can help manage ADHD symptoms.

43. Baked Sweet Potato with Black Bean Salsa

Ingredients:
For the Sweet Potatoes:
- 4 medium-sized sweet potatoes
- 1 tablespoon olive oil
- Salt and pepper to taste

For the Black Bean Salsa:
- 1 can (15 ounces) black beans, drained and rinsed
- 1/2 cup diced red onion
- 1 cup diced tomatoes
- 1/4 cup chopped fresh cilantro
- Juice of 1 lime
- 1 tablespoon olive oil
- Salt and pepper to taste
- Optional toppings: avocado slices, Greek yogurt or sour cream, shredded cheese

Instructions:
- Preheat your oven to 400°F (200°C).

- Scrub the sweet potatoes clean and pat them dry with a paper towel. Prick the sweet potatoes several times with a fork or knife. Rub the sweet potatoes with olive oil and season them with salt and pepper.

- Place the sweet potatoes on a baking sheet lined with parchment paper or aluminum foil.

- Bake the sweet potatoes in the preheated oven for 45-60 minutes, or until they are tender and can be easily pierced with a fork.

- While the sweet potatoes are baking, prepare the black bean salsa. In a mixing bowl, combine the black beans, diced tomatoes, red onion, cilantro, lime juice, olive oil, salt, and pepper. Stir until well combined. Adjust seasoning to taste.

- Once the sweet potatoes are done baking, remove them from the oven and let them cool slightly.

- To serve, slice each sweet potato lengthwise and fluff the flesh with a fork. Top each sweet potato with a generous spoonful of black bean salsa.

- Garnish with optional toppings such as avocado slices, Greek yogurt or sour cream, and shredded cheese, if desired. Serve the baked sweet potatoes with black bean salsa immediately.

This dish is not only delicious but also packed with nutrients. It provides a balance of complex carbohydrates, fiber, protein, and healthy fats, which can help support brain health and manage ADHD symptoms. Enjoy!

44. Tuna Salad Lettuce Wraps

Ingredients:
For the Tuna Salad:
- 2 cans (5 ounces each) tuna, drained
- 1/4 cup mayonnaise
- 2 tablespoons Greek yogurt (or sour cream)
- 2 tablespoons diced red onion
- 2 tablespoons diced celery
- 1 tablespoon chopped fresh parsley (optional)
- 1 tablespoon lemon juice
- Salt and pepper to taste

For the Lettuce Wraps:
- Large lettuce leaves (such as romaine or butter lettuce)
- Optional toppings: sliced avocado, diced tomatoes, shredded carrots, cucumber slices

Instructions:
- In a mixing bowl, combine the drained tuna, mayonnaise, Greek yogurt, diced red onion, diced celery, chopped fresh parsley (if using), lemon juice, salt, and pepper. Stir until well combined.

- Taste the tuna salad and adjust seasoning if necessary. Add more mayonnaise or Greek yogurt for creaminess, if desired.

- Wash and dry the lettuce leaves. Pat them gently with a paper towel to remove excess moisture.

- Spoon a portion of the tuna salad onto each lettuce leaf, towards the bottom end.

- Add optional toppings such as sliced avocado, diced tomatoes, shredded carrots, or cucumber slices on top of the tuna salad.

- Roll up the lettuce leaves, starting from the bottom, to form wraps.

- Secure the wraps with toothpicks if needed.

- Serve the tuna salad lettuce wraps immediately, or refrigerate them for later.

These tuna salad lettuce wraps are low in carbs and high in protein, making them a nutritious option for a quick and easy meal. Plus, the omega-3 fatty acids from the tuna can help support brain health. Enjoy!

45. Spinach and Mushroom Quiche

Ingredients:
For the Crust:
- 1 1/4 cups all-purpose flour
- 1/2 teaspoon salt
- 1/2 cup cold unsalted butter,
cut into small pieces
- 3-4 tablespoons ice water

For the Filling:
- 1 tablespoon olive oil

- 8 ounces mushrooms, sliced
- 2 cups fresh spinach leaves
- 4 large eggs
- 1 cup milk (or half-and-half for a richer quiche)
- 1/2 cup shredded cheese (such as Swiss, GruyÃre, or cheddar)
- Salt and pepper to taste
- Pinch of nutmeg (optional)
- Chopped fresh herbs for garnish (optional)
- 1 small onion, diced

Instructions:
- Preheat your oven to 375Â°F (190Â°C).

- In a mixing bowl, combine the flour and salt for the crust. Add the cold butter pieces and use a pastry cutter or fork to cut the butter into the flour until the mixture resembles coarse crumbs.

- Gradually add the ice water, one tablespoon at a time, and mix until the dough comes together. Be careful not to overwork the dough. Shape the dough into a disk, wrap it in plastic wrap, and refrigerate for at least 30 minutes.

- While the dough is chilling, heat the olive oil in a skillet over medium heat. Add the diced onion and cook until softened, about 3-4 minutes. Add the sliced mushrooms to the skillet and cook until they release their moisture and are tender, about 5-6 minutes.

- Add the fresh spinach leaves to the skillet and cook until wilted, about 2-3 minutes. Remove the skillet from the heat and let the mixture cool slightly. In a separate mixing bowl, whisk together the eggs and milk until well combined. Season with salt, pepper, and a pinch of nutmeg, if using.

- Roll out the chilled dough on a floured surface to fit a 9-inch pie dish. Carefully transfer the dough to the pie dish and press it into the bottom and sides. Spread the mushroom and spinach mixture evenly over the bottom of the pie crust. Sprinkle shredded cheese on top.

- Pour the egg mixture over the filling in the pie crust. Bake the quiche in the preheated oven for 35-40 minutes, or suntil the filling is set and the crust is golden brown. Remove the quiche from the oven and let it cool for a few minutes before slicing. Garnish with chopped fresh herbs, if desired, before serving.

46. Mediterranean Veggie Wrap

Ingredients:
For the Wrap: 1 large whole wheat or spinach tortilla wrap

For the Filling:
- 1/4 cup hummus (store-bought or homemade)
- 1/2 cup mixed salad greens (such as spinach, arugula, or lettuce)
- 1/4 cup sliced cucumbers
- 1/4 cup sliced bell peppers (any color)
- 1/4 cup sliced tomatoes
- 1/4 cup sliced red onions
- 2-3 tablespoons crumbled feta cheese
- 2 tablespoons sliced Kalamata olives
- Optional: sliced avocado, chopped fresh parsley or cilantro

Instructions:
- Lay the tortilla wrap flat on a clean surface.

- Spread the hummus evenly over the surface of the tortilla, leaving a small border around the edges.

- Layer the mixed salad greens, sliced cucumbers, bell peppers, tomatoes, and red onions on top of the hummus.

- Sprinkle crumbled feta cheese and sliced Kalamata olives over the veggies.

- If desired, add sliced avocado and chopped fresh herbs for extra flavor.

- Roll up the tortilla tightly, tucking in the sides as you go, to form a wrap.

- Cut the wrap in half diagonally, if desired, for easier handling.

- Serve immediately, or wrap in parchment paper or foil for a portable meal.

This Mediterranean veggie wrap is not only colorful and flavorful but also provides a good balance of carbohydrates, fiber, vitamins, and minerals. It's a great option for a healthy lunch or snack to keep you fueled and focused throughout the day. Enjoy!

47. Cauliflower Mash

Ingredients:
- 1 large head of cauliflower, cut into florets
- 2-3 cloves garlic, minced
- 2 tablespoons unsalted butter or olive oil
- 1/4 cup grated Parmesan cheese (optional)
- Salt and pepper to taste
- Chopped fresh herbs for garnish (such as parsley or chives)

Instructions:

- Bring a large pot of salted water to a boil. Add the cauliflower florets and minced garlic to the pot.

- Boil the cauliflower for 8-10 minutes, or until it is fork-tender.

- Drain the cauliflower and garlic, then transfer them to a large mixing bowl.

- Using a potato masher or a hand blender, mash the cauliflower and garlic until smooth. Alternatively, you can use a food processor for a smoother texture.

- Add the unsalted butter or olive oil to the mashed cauliflower and mix until well combined.

- If using, stir in the grated Parmesan cheese for extra flavor.

- Season the cauliflower mash with salt and pepper to taste. Adjust seasoning as needed.

- Transfer the cauliflower mash to a serving dish and garnish with chopped fresh herbs.

- Serve the cauliflower mash hot as a side dish alongside your favorite protein or vegetable dishes.

This cauliflower mash is creamy, flavorful, and satisfying. It's a great way to incorporate more vegetables into your diet while still enjoying a comforting and familiar dish. Plus, the cauliflower provides essential nutrients like vitamin C and folate, which can help support brain health and cognitive function. Enjoy!

48. Black Bean and Corn Salad

Ingredients:
- 1 can (15 ounces) black beans, drained and rinsed
- 1 cup frozen corn kernels, thawed
- 1/2 red bell pepper, diced
- 1/2 green bell pepper, diced
- 1/4 cup diced red onion
- 1/4 cup chopped fresh cilantro
- Juice of 1 lime
- 2 tablespoons olive oil
- 1 teaspoon ground cumin
- 1/2 teaspoon chili powder
- Salt and pepper to taste
- Optional: diced avocado, cherry tomatoes, jalapeÃ±o peppers for extra flavor and heat

Instructions:
- In a large mixing bowl, combine the black beans, thawed corn kernels, diced red and green bell peppers, diced red onion, and chopped fresh cilantro.

- In a small bowl, whisk together the lime juice, olive oil, ground cumin, chili powder, salt, and pepper to make the dressing.

- Pour the dressing over the black bean and corn mixture, and toss until everything is well coated.

- Taste the salad and adjust seasoning as needed. Add more lime juice, salt, or pepper if desired.

- If using, gently fold in diced avocado, halved cherry tomatoes, or sliced jalapeÃ±o peppers for extra flavor and heat.

- Cover the bowl with plastic wrap and refrigerate the black bean and corn salad for at least 30 minutes to allow the flavors to meld.

- Before serving, give the salad a quick toss to redistribute the dressing.

- Serve the black bean and corn salad chilled as a side dish or a light meal.

This black bean and corn salad is not only vibrant and flavorful but also packed with protein, fiber, and essential nutrients. It's a great option for a quick and nutritious meal that can help support brain health and cognitive function. Enjoy!

49. Greek Chicken Souvlaki

Ingredients:

For Serving:
- Pita bread or flatbread
- Tzatziki sauce
(store-bought or homemade)
- Sliced tomatoes
- Sliced red onions
- Chopped fresh parsley or
cilantro for garnish

For the Chicken Marinade:
- 1.5 lbs (about 700g) boneless, skinless chicken breasts, cut into bite-sized pieces
- 1/4 cup olive oil
- Juice of 1 lemon
- 3 cloves garlic, minced
- 1 teaspoon dried oregano
- 1 teaspoon dried thyme
- 1/2 teaspoon dried rosemary
- Salt and pepper to taste

Instructions:
- In a mixing bowl, combine the olive oil, lemon juice, minced garlic, dried oregano, dried thyme, dried rosemary, salt, and pepper to make the marinade.

- Add the chicken pieces to the marinade and toss until they are well coated. Cover the bowl and refrigerate for at least 30 minutes, or up to 4 hours, to allow the flavors to meld.

- Preheat your grill or grill pan over medium-high heat. Thread the marinated chicken pieces onto skewers, leaving a little space between each piece.

- Grill the chicken skewers for 4-5 minutes per side, or until they are cooked through and have nice grill marks.

- While the chicken is grilling, warm the pita bread or flatbread on the grill for 1-2 minutes on each side, until lightly toasted and warmed through.

- Once the chicken skewers are done cooking, remove them from the grill and let them rest for a few minutes.

- To serve, place a few pieces of grilled chicken onto each warmed pita bread or flatbread. Top with sliced tomatoes, sliced red onions, and a dollop of tzatziki sauce. Garnish with chopped fresh parsley or cilantro. Roll up the pita bread or flatbread to form wraps, and serve immediately.

This Greek chicken souvlaki is bursting with Mediterranean flavors and is sure to satisfy your taste buds. Plus, it's packed with lean protein, which can help support brain health and cognitive function. Enjoy this delicious and nutritious meal!

50. Stuffed Portobello Mushrooms

Ingredients:
- 4 large Portobello mushrooms, stems removed and cleaned
- 1 tablespoon olive oil
- 2 cloves garlic, minced
- 1/2 small onion, finely diced
- 1 cup fresh spinach, chopped
- 1/2 cup sun-dried tomatoes, chopped
- 1/2 cup crumbled feta cheese (or cheese of your choice)
- 1/4 cup grated Parmesan cheese
- Salt and pepper to taste
- Optional toppings: chopped fresh herbs (such as parsley or basil), balsamic glaze

Instructions:
- Preheat your oven to 375Â°F (190Â°C).

- In a skillet, heat the olive oil over medium heat. Add the minced garlic and diced onion, and sautÃ© until softened, about 2-3 minutes.

- Add the chopped spinach to the skillet and cook until wilted, about 2 minutes. Remove from heat and set aside.

- Place the cleaned Portobello mushrooms on a baking sheet lined with parchment paper or aluminum foil, gill-side up.

- Divide the sautÃ©ed spinach mixture evenly among the mushrooms, pressing it gently into each cap.

- Top each mushroom with chopped sun-dried tomatoes, crumbled feta cheese, and grated Parmesan cheese. Season the stuffed mushrooms with salt and pepper to taste.

- Bake in the preheated oven for 20-25 minutes, or until the mushrooms are tender and the cheese is melted and bubbly.

- Remove the stuffed mushrooms from the oven and let them cool for a few minutes. Garnish with chopped fresh herbs and drizzle with balsamic glaze, if desired, before serving.

These stuffed Portobello mushrooms are flavorful, satisfying, and packed with nutrients. They can be served as a vegetarian main course or as a side dish alongside your favorite protein. Enjoy this delicious and nutritious meal!

51. Spicy Peanut Noodles with Tofu

Ingredients:

For the Peanut Sauce:

- 1/4 cup creamy peanut butter
- 2 tablespoons soy sauce
(or tamari for gluten-free)
- 2 tablespoons rice vinegar
- 1 tablespoon sesame oil
- 1 tablespoon honey
(or maple syrup for vegan)
- 1 clove garlic, minced
- 1 teaspoon grated fresh ginger
- 1/2 teaspoon crushed red
pepper flakes (adjust to taste)
- 2-4 tablespoons water, to thin the sauce

For the Noodles and Tofu:

- 8 ounces (about 225g) whole wheat spaghetti or rice noodles
- 1 tablespoon sesame oil
- 14 ounces (about 400g) firm tofu, drained and cubed
- Salt and pepper to taste
- 1 red bell pepper, thinly sliced
- 1 cup shredded carrots
- 2 green onions, thinly sliced
- Optional garnishes: chopped peanuts, sesame seeds, cilantro, lime wedges

Instructions:

- Cook the noodles according to the package instructions until al dente. Drain and set aside.

- In a small bowl, whisk together all the ingredients for the peanut sauce until smooth. Add more water, if needed, to achieve your desired consistency. Set aside.

- Heat the sesame oil in a large skillet or wok over medium-high heat. Add the cubed tofu to the skillet and season with salt and pepper. Cook until the tofu is golden brown on all sides, about 8-10 minutes. Remove the tofu from the skillet and set aside.

- In the same skillet, add the sliced bell pepper and shredded carrots. Stir-fry for 2-3 minutes, or until the vegetables are tender-crisp.

- Return the cooked noodles and tofu to the skillet. Pour the peanut sauce over the noodles and tofu, and toss until everything is evenly coated and heated through. Remove the skillet from the heat and stir in the sliced green onions.

- Divide the spicy peanut noodles with tofu among serving plates. Garnish with chopped peanuts, sesame seeds, cilantro, and lime wedges, if desired. Serve immediately and enjoy!

These spicy peanut noodles with tofu are packed with flavor and nutrients, making them a satisfying and wholesome meal. Plus, the combination of protein, healthy fats, and complex carbohydrates can help support brain health and cognitive function. Enjoy this delicious and nutritious dish!

52. Baked Chicken Fajitas

Ingredients:
- 1 lb (about 450g) boneless, skinless chicken breasts, thinly sliced
- 2 bell peppers (any color), thinly sliced
- 1 large onion, thinly sliced
- 2 tablespoons olive oil
- 1 packet (about 1.25 ounces) fajita seasoning mix (or make your own with chili powder, cumin, paprika, garlic powder, onion powder, salt, and pepper)
- Juice of 1 lime
- Optional toppings: sliced avocado, sour cream, shredded cheese, chopped cilantro, salsa
- Flour or corn tortillas for serving

Instructions:

- Preheat your oven to 400Â°F (200Â°C).

- In a large mixing bowl, combine the thinly sliced chicken breasts, sliced bell peppers, sliced onion, olive oil, fajita seasoning mix, and lime juice. Toss until everything is evenly coated.
- Transfer the chicken and vegetable mixture to a large baking dish or sheet pan, spreading it out into an even layer.

- Bake in the preheated oven for 20-25 minutes, or until the chicken is cooked through and the vegetables are tender.

- While the chicken and vegetables are baking, warm the tortillas in a dry skillet or in the microwave.

- Once the chicken and vegetables are done baking, remove them from the oven and serve immediately.

- Allow each person to assemble their own fajitas by spooning some of the chicken and vegetable mixture onto a warm tortilla. Top with optional toppings such as sliced avocado, sour cream, shredded cheese, chopped cilantro, and salsa.

- Roll up the tortillas and enjoy your delicious baked chicken fajitas!

These baked chicken fajitas are not only flavorful and satisfying but also easy to customize based on personal preferences. Plus, they provide a good balance of protein, fiber, and healthy fats, which can help support brain health and cognitive function. Enjoy this tasty and nutritious meal!

53. Lentil and Spinach Salad with Feta

Ingredients:
For the Salad:
- 1 cup dried green lentils, rinsed and drained
- 3 cups fresh spinach leaves, chopped
- 1/2 red onion, thinly sliced
- 1/2 cup crumbled feta cheese
- 1/4 cup chopped fresh parsley
- 1/4 cup chopped fresh cilantro
- Optional: sliced cherry tomatoes, sliced cucumber, diced bell peppers

For the Dressing:
- 3 tablespoons extra virgin olive oil
- 2 tablespoons balsamic vinegar
- 1 tablespoon Dijon mustard
- 1 clove garlic, minced
- Salt and pepper to taste

Instructions:
- In a medium saucepan, combine the dried lentils with 2 cups of water. Bring to a boil, then reduce the heat to low and simmer, covered, for 20-25 minutes, or until the lentils are tender but still firm. Drain any excess water and let the lentils cool slightly.

- In a large mixing bowl, combine the cooked lentils, chopped spinach leaves, thinly sliced red onion, crumbled feta cheese, chopped fresh parsley, and chopped fresh cilantro. Add any optional ingredients, such as sliced cherry tomatoes, sliced cucumber, or diced bell peppers, if desired.

- In a small bowl, whisk together the extra virgin olive oil, balsamic vinegar, Dijon mustard, minced garlic, salt, and pepper to make the dressing.

- Pour the dressing over the lentil and spinach mixture in the large mixing bowl. Toss until everything is evenly coated with the dressing.

- Taste the salad and adjust seasoning as needed. Serve the lentil and spinach salad with feta immediately, or refrigerate for at least 30 minutes to allow the flavors to meld before serving.

This lentil and spinach salad with feta is not only delicious and satisfying but also nutritious and supportive for managing ADHD symptoms. It's a great option for a quick and easy meal that's packed with plant-based protein and fiber. Enjoy this flavorful and wholesome dish!

54. Coconut Curry Chicken

Ingredients:

- 1 lb (about 450g) boneless, skinless chicken breasts, cut into bite-sized pieces
- 1 tablespoon coconut oil
- 1 onion, finely chopped
- 3 cloves garlic, minced
- 1 tablespoon grated fresh ginger
- 2 tablespoons curry powder
- 1 can (13.5 ounces) coconut milk
- 1 cup chicken broth
- 2 cups mixed vegetables (such as bell peppers, carrots, peas, and broccoli)
- Salt and pepper to taste
- Optional toppings: chopped fresh cilantro, sliced green onions, lime wedges

Instructions:

- In a large skillet or Dutch oven, heat the coconut oil over medium heat. Add the chopped onion and cook until softened, about 3-4 minutes.

- Add the minced garlic and grated fresh ginger to the skillet, and cook for another 1-2 minutes, until fragrant.

- Stir in the curry powder and cook for 1 minute, until toasted and aromatic.

- Add the bite-sized chicken pieces to the skillet and cook until they are browned on all sides, about 5-6 minutes.

- Pour in the coconut milk and chicken broth, and stir to combine. Bring the mixture to a simmer.

- Add the mixed vegetables to the skillet, and stir to combine. Cover the skillet and let the curry simmer for 10-15 minutes, or until the chicken is cooked through and the vegetables are tender.

- Taste the curry and season with salt and pepper to taste. Adjust seasoning as needed.

- Serve the coconut curry chicken hot, garnished with chopped fresh cilantro, sliced green onions, and lime wedges, if desired.

- Serve the coconut curry chicken over cooked rice or quinoa, if desired, for a complete meal.

This coconut curry chicken is rich, creamy, and packed with flavor, making it a satisfying and nutritious meal option. Plus, it's easy to customize with your favorite vegetables and spices. Enjoy this delicious and comforting dish!

55. Quinoa and Black Bean Stuffed Bell Peppers

Ingredients:
* 4 large bell peppers (any color), halved and seeds removed
* 1 cup quinoa, rinsed
* 2 cups vegetable broth or water
* 1 can (15 ounces) black beans, drained and rinsed
* 1 cup corn kernels (fresh, frozen, or canned)
* 1 cup diced tomatoes (fresh or canned)
* 1/2 cup diced red onion
* 2 cloves garlic, minced
* 1 teaspoon ground cumin
* 1 teaspoon chili powder
* Salt and pepper to taste
* 1 cup shredded cheese (such as cheddar or pepper jack)
* Optional toppings: chopped fresh cilantro, sliced avocado, Greek yogurt or sour cream

Instructions:
* Preheat your oven to 375°F (190°C). Lightly grease a baking dish large enough to hold the bell pepper halves.

* In a medium saucepan, bring the vegetable broth or water to a boil. Add the quinoa, reduce the heat to low, cover, and simmer for 15-20 minutes, or until the quinoa is cooked and the liquid is absorbed.

* In a large mixing bowl, combine the cooked quinoa, black beans, corn kernels, diced tomatoes, diced red onion, minced garlic, ground cumin, chili powder, salt, and pepper. Stir until everything is well mixed.

* Arrange the bell pepper halves in the prepared baking dish, cut side up. Spoon the quinoa and black bean mixture evenly into each bell pepper half, pressing down gently to pack the filling.

* Cover the baking dish with aluminum foil and bake in the preheated oven for 25-30 minutes, or until the bell peppers are tender.

* Remove the foil from the baking dish and sprinkle the shredded cheese evenly over the stuffed bell peppers.

* Return the baking dish to the oven and bake for an additional 5-10 minutes, or until the cheese is melted and bubbly.

* Remove the stuffed bell peppers from the oven and let them cool for a few minutes before serving.

* Garnish the stuffed bell peppers with optional toppings such as chopped fresh cilantro, sliced avocado, and Greek yogurt or sour cream.

56. Balsamic Glazed Salmon

Ingredients:
- 4 salmon fillets (about 6 ounces each)
- Salt and pepper to taste
- 2 tablespoons olive oil
- 1/4 cup balsamic vinegar
- 2 tablespoons honey (or maple syrup for a vegan option)
- 2 cloves garlic, minced
- 1 teaspoon dried thyme (or 1 tablespoon chopped fresh thyme)
- Optional garnish: chopped fresh parsley or green onions

Instructions:
- Preheat your oven to 400°F (200°C). Line a baking sheet with parchment paper or aluminum foil for easy cleanup.

- Season the salmon fillets with salt and pepper to taste on both sides.

- In a small saucepan, combine the balsamic vinegar, honey, minced garlic, and dried thyme. Bring the mixture to a simmer over medium heat, then reduce the heat to low and simmer for 5-7 minutes, or until the glaze has thickened slightly.

- While the glaze is simmering, heat the olive oil in a large oven-safe skillet over medium-high heat. Once hot, add the salmon fillets to the skillet, skin-side down, and sear for 2-3 minutes, or until golden brown.

- Carefully flip the salmon fillets over using a spatula, then brush the tops generously with the balsamic glaze.

- Transfer the skillet to the preheated oven and bake for 8-10 minutes, or until the salmon is cooked through and flakes easily with a fork.

- Remove the skillet from the oven and brush the salmon fillets with any remaining glaze from the saucepan.

- Serve the balsamic glazed salmon hot, garnished with chopped fresh parsley or green onions, if desired.

This balsamic glazed salmon is not only delicious and flavorful but also packed with heart-healthy omega-3 fatty acids and protein. It's a nutritious and satisfying dish that's perfect for a quick weeknight dinner or a special occasion meal. Enjoy this tasty and wholesome dish!

57. Thai Coconut Soup with Shrimp

Ingredients:

- 1 tablespoon coconut oil or vegetable oil
- 1 small onion, thinly sliced
- 2 cloves garlic, minced
- 1 tablespoon grated fresh ginger
- 2 lemongrass stalks, bruised and chopped into pieces
- 3 cups chicken or vegetable broth
- 1 can (13.5 ounces) coconut milk
- 1 tablespoon fish sauce (or soy sauce for a vegetarian option)
- 1 tablespoon lime juice
- 1 tablespoon brown sugar (or palm sugar)
- 1-2 Thai bird's eye chilies, thinly sliced (adjust to taste)
- 1 cup sliced mushrooms (such as straw mushrooms or button mushrooms)
- 1 lb (about 450g) shrimp, peeled and deveined
- Salt and pepper to taste
- 3-4 kaffir lime leaves (optional)
- Chopped fresh cilantro for garnish
- Thinly sliced red chili for garnish (optional)

Instructions:

- In a large pot or Dutch oven, heat the coconut oil over medium heat. Add the sliced onion, minced garlic, and grated fresh ginger, and sauté for 2-3 minutes until fragrant.

- Add the bruised lemongrass stalks and kaffir lime leaves (if using) to the pot, and sauté for another minute.

- Pour in the chicken or vegetable broth and bring the mixture to a simmer. Let it simmer for 5-10 minutes to allow the flavors to infuse.

- Stir in the coconut milk, fish sauce (or soy sauce), lime juice, brown sugar (or palm sugar), and sliced Thai bird's eye chilies. Let the soup simmer for another 5 minutes.

- Add the sliced mushrooms to the pot and simmer for 3-4 minutes, or until the mushrooms are tender. Stir in the peeled and deveined shrimp and cook for 3-4 minutes, or until the shrimp are pink and cooked through.

- Taste the soup and adjust seasoning with salt, pepper, and additional lime juice or fish sauce as needed. Remove the pot from the heat and discard the lemongrass stalks and kaffir lime leaves.

- Ladle the Thai coconut soup with shrimp into serving bowls. Garnish with chopped fresh cilantro and thinly sliced red chili, if desired. Serve the soup hot as a comforting and flavorful meal.

This Thai coconut soup with shrimp is fragrant, creamy, and bursting with flavors of lemongrass, coconut, and spices. It's a comforting and satisfying dish that's perfect for any occasion. Enjoy this delicious and wholesome soup!

58. Veggie Frittata

Ingredients:
- 8 large eggs
- 1/4 cup milk (or non-dairy milk)
- Salt and pepper to taste
- 1 tablespoon olive oil
- 1 small onion, diced
- 1 bell pepper, diced
- 1 cup diced vegetables (such as spinach, mushrooms, zucchini, or tomatoes)
- 1/2 cup shredded cheese (such as cheddar, mozzarella, or feta)
- Optional add-ins: cooked diced ham, cooked crumbled bacon, cooked sausage, or cooked quinoa

Instructions:
- Preheat your oven to 350Â°F (175Â°C).

- In a large mixing bowl, whisk together the eggs, milk, salt, and pepper until well combined. Set aside.

- Heat the olive oil in a large oven-safe skillet over medium heat. Add the diced onion and bell pepper, and sautÃ© until softened, about 5 minutes.

- Add the diced vegetables to the skillet and cook for another 3-4 minutes, or until they are tender.

- If using any optional add-ins like cooked meat or quinoa, add them to the skillet and stir to combine with the vegetables.

- Pour the egg mixture evenly over the vegetables and optional add-ins in the skillet. Sprinkle the shredded cheese evenly over the top. Cook the frittata on the stovetop for 3-4 minutes, or until the edges start to set.

- Transfer the skillet to the preheated oven and bake the frittata for 15-20 minutes, or until the eggs are set and the top is golden brown.

- Remove the skillet from the oven and let the frittata cool for a few minutes before slicing. Slice the frittata into wedges and serve hot, warm, or at room temperature.

This veggie frittata is not only delicious and satisfying but also packed with protein, vitamins, and minerals from the eggs and vegetables. It's a great way to use up leftover vegetables and customize the frittata based on personal preferences. Enjoy this nutritious and versatile dish for breakfast, brunch, lunch, or dinner!

59. Caprese Stuffed Avocados

Ingredients:
- 2 ripe avocados, halved and pits removed
- 1 cup cherry tomatoes, halved
- 1/2 cup fresh mozzarella balls (or diced mozzarella)
- 1/4 cup fresh basil leaves, thinly sliced
- 2 tablespoons balsamic glaze
- Salt and pepper to taste
- Optional garnish: extra basil leaves, cracked black pepper

Instructions:

- Scoop out a small portion of the flesh from each avocado half to create a larger cavity for the filling. Reserve the scooped-out avocado flesh for another use or mash it and add it to the filling mixture.

- In a mixing bowl, combine the cherry tomatoes, fresh mozzarella balls, and thinly sliced basil leaves.

- Drizzle the balsamic glaze over the tomato and mozzarella mixture, and gently toss to coat.

- Season the mixture with salt and pepper to taste, adjusting seasoning as needed.

- Spoon the tomato and mozzarella mixture evenly into the cavities of the avocado halves, pressing down gently to pack the filling.

- Drizzle a little more balsamic glaze over the stuffed avocados for extra flavor, if desired.

- Garnish the stuffed avocados with extra basil leaves and cracked black pepper, if desired.

- Serve the Caprese stuffed avocados immediately as a delicious and nutritious appetizer or light meal.

These Caprese stuffed avocados are not only visually appealing but also packed with flavor and nutrients. They make for a satisfying and wholesome dish that's perfect for any occasion. Enjoy this simple and delicious recipe!

60. Grilled Vegetable Platter with Hummus

Ingredients:
For the Grilled Vegetables:
- 2 zucchinis, sliced lengthwise into strips
- 2 bell peppers (any color), sliced into quarters
- 1 eggplant, sliced into rounds
- 1 red onion, sliced into rounds
- 1 tablespoon olive oil
- Salt and pepper to taste
- Optional: other vegetables such as
mushrooms, cherry tomatoes, asparagus, or carrots

For the Hummus:
- 1 can (15 ounces) chickpeas, drained and rinsed
- 2 cloves garlic, minced
- 2 tablespoons tahini
- Juice of 1 lemon
- 2 tablespoons olive oil
- Salt to taste
- Water, as needed to adjust consistency

Instructions:
- Preheat your grill or grill pan to medium-high heat.

- In a large mixing bowl, toss the sliced zucchinis, bell peppers, eggplant, and red onion with olive oil, salt, and pepper until evenly coated.

For Serving:
- Fresh herbs for garnish (such as parsley, cilantro, or mint)
- Lemon wedges

- Grill the vegetables in batches, arranging them in a single layer on the grill. Grill for 3-4 minutes per side, or until they are tender and have grill marks.

- While the vegetables are grilling, prepare the hummus. In a food processor, combine the chickpeas, minced garlic, tahini, lemon juice, olive oil, and salt. Blend until smooth, adding water as needed to achieve your desired consistency. Taste and adjust seasoning as needed.

- Arrange the grilled vegetables on a large platter. Serve the hummus alongside the grilled vegetables.

- Garnish the platter with fresh herbs and lemon wedges.

- Serve the grilled vegetable platter with hummus as a delicious and nutritious appetizer, side dish, or light meal.

This grilled vegetable platter with hummus is not only visually stunning but also packed with flavor and nutrients. It's a great way to enjoy seasonal vegetables and provide a variety of textures and flavors in one dish. Enjoy this vibrant and wholesome recipe!

61. Turkey and Quinoa Meatloaf

Ingredients:

- 1 lb (about 450g) ground turkey
- 1 cup cooked quinoa
- 1 small onion, finely chopped
- 2 cloves garlic, minced
- 1/2 cup grated carrots
- 1/2 cup grated zucchini
- 1/4 cup chopped fresh parsley
- 1/4 cup tomato sauce
- 1 tablespoon Worcestershire sauce (optional)
- 1 teaspoon dried thyme
- 1 teaspoon dried oregano
- Salt and pepper to taste
- 1/4 cup ketchup or barbecue sauce (for topping)

Instructions:

- Preheat your oven to 375Â°F (190Â°C). Lightly grease a loaf pan or line it with parchment paper.

- In a large mixing bowl, combine the ground turkey, cooked quinoa, chopped onion, minced garlic, grated carrots, grated zucchini, chopped parsley, tomato sauce, Worcestershire sauce (if using), dried thyme, dried oregano, salt, and pepper. Mix until everything is well combined.

- Transfer the turkey and quinoa mixture to the prepared loaf pan, pressing it down evenly.

- Spread the ketchup or barbecue sauce evenly over the top of the meatloaf.

- Bake the meatloaf in the preheated oven for 45-55 minutes, or until it is cooked through and the top is golden brown.

- Remove the meatloaf from the oven and let it rest for a few minutes before slicing.

- Slice the turkey and quinoa meatloaf into thick slices and serve hot.

This turkey and quinoa meatloaf is not only delicious and satisfying but also packed with lean protein, whole grains, and vegetables. It's a wholesome and balanced meal that's perfect for a family dinner or meal prep. Enjoy this nutritious and flavorful recipe!

62. Zucchini Lasagna

Ingredients:

- 1 teaspoon dried basil
- 1 teaspoon dried oregano
- Salt and pepper to taste
- 2 cups ricotta cheese
- 1/2 cup grated Parmesan cheese
- 2 cups shredded mozzarella cheese
- Fresh basil leaves for garnish (optional)
- 4 medium zucchinis, sliced lengthwise into thin strips (about 1/4 inch thick)
- 1 tablespoon olive oil
- 1 onion, finely chopped
- 3 cloves garlic, minced
- 1 lb (about 450g) ground turkey or lean ground beef (optional)
- 1 can (24 ounces) crushed tomatoes

Instructions:

- Preheat your oven to 375Â°F (190Â°C). Lightly grease a 9x13-inch baking dish with olive oil or cooking spray.

- Heat the olive oil in a large skillet over medium heat. Add the chopped onion and minced garlic, and sautÃ© until softened, about 3-4 minutes.

- If using ground turkey or lean ground beef, add it to the skillet with the onion and garlic. Cook until browned and cooked through, breaking it up with a spoon as it cooks.

- Stir in the crushed tomatoes, dried basil, dried oregano, salt, and pepper. Simmer the sauce for 10-15 minutes, stirring occasionally, to allow the flavors to meld.

- While the sauce is simmering, prepare the zucchini strips. Use a mandoline slicer or a sharp knife to slice the zucchinis lengthwise into thin strips. In a small bowl, combine the ricotta cheese and grated Parmesan cheese.

- To assemble the lasagna, spread a thin layer of the tomato sauce in the bottom of the prepared baking dish. Arrange a layer of zucchini strips on top of the sauce, overlapping slightly to cover the bottom of the dish.

- Spread half of the ricotta cheese mixture over the zucchini layer, followed by a layer of shredded mozzarella cheese. Repeat the layers with the remaining sauce, zucchini strips, ricotta mixture, and shredded mozzarella cheese, ending with a layer of cheese on top.
- Cover the baking dish with aluminum foil and bake in the preheated oven for 30 minutes.

- Remove the foil from the baking dish and bake the lasagna for an additional 15-20 minutes, or until the cheese is golden brown and bubbly.

- Remove the lasagna from the oven and let it cool for a few minutes before slicing. Garnish the zucchini lasagna with fresh basil leaves, if desired, and serve hot.

63. Chicken and Avocado Wrap

Ingredients:
- 2 large whole wheat or spinach tortillas
- 1 cup cooked chicken breast, shredded or thinly sliced
- 1 ripe avocado, thinly sliced
- 1/2 cup shredded lettuce or spinach leaves
- 1/4 cup diced tomatoes
- 2 tablespoons diced red onion
- 2 tablespoons chopped fresh cilantro (optional)
- 1/4 cup Greek yogurt or sour cream
- 1 tablespoon lime juice
- Salt and pepper to taste
- Hot sauce or salsa (optional)

Instructions:

- In a small bowl, combine the Greek yogurt or sour cream with lime juice, chopped cilantro (if using), salt, and pepper to make a creamy dressing. Set aside.

- Lay out the tortillas on a clean work surface.

- Divide the shredded chicken evenly between the two tortillas, spreading it out in the center of each tortilla.

- Top the chicken with sliced avocado, shredded lettuce or spinach leaves, diced tomatoes, and diced red onion.

- Drizzle the creamy dressing over the fillings on each tortilla.

- If desired, add a few dashes of hot sauce or salsa for extra flavor.

- Fold the sides of each tortilla over the fillings, then roll them up tightly to form wraps.

- Slice the wraps in half diagonally, if desired, and serve immediately.

These chicken and avocado wraps are not only delicious and filling but also packed with protein, healthy fats, and fiber. They make for a perfect on-the-go meal or a quick lunch or dinner option. Enjoy this tasty and nutritious recipe!

64. Egg Drop Soup

Ingredients:
- 4 cups chicken or vegetable broth
- 2 eggs
- 2 green onions, thinly sliced
- 1 tablespoon soy sauce (or tamari for gluten-free)
- 1 teaspoon sesame oil
- 1/2 teaspoon grated fresh ginger
- Salt and pepper to taste
- Optional: sliced mushrooms, diced tofu, shredded cooked chicken, or cooked shrimp

Instructions:
- In a medium saucepan, bring the chicken or vegetable broth to a simmer over medium heat.

- While the broth is heating, whisk the eggs in a small bowl until well beaten.

- Once the broth is simmering, stir in the sliced green onions, soy sauce, sesame oil, and grated fresh ginger. Add any optional ingredients such as sliced mushrooms, diced tofu, shredded cooked chicken, or cooked shrimp, if desired.

- Slowly pour the beaten eggs into the simmering broth in a steady stream while stirring the soup gently with a fork or chopsticks. The eggs will cook and form delicate ribbons as they mix with the hot broth.

- Continue to cook the soup for another 1-2 minutes, or until the eggs are fully cooked and the soup is heated through.

- Taste the soup and adjust seasoning with salt and pepper as needed.

- Remove the soup from the heat and ladle it into serving bowls.

- Garnish the egg drop soup with additional sliced green onions, if desired, and serve hot.

This egg drop soup is not only comforting and delicious but also packed with protein and essential nutrients. It's a simple and satisfying meal option that can be enjoyed on its own or paired with a side of steamed rice or crusty bread. Enjoy this nourishing and flavorful recipe!

65. Spaghetti Squash Pad Thai

Ingredients:

- 1 medium spaghetti squash
- 2 tablespoons olive oil
- 2 cloves garlic, minced
- 1 small onion, thinly sliced
- 1 red bell pepper, thinly sliced
- 1 carrot, julienned
- 1 cup broccoli florets
- 2 eggs, beaten
- 1/4 cup chopped peanuts or cashews
- 2 green onions, thinly sliced
- 1/4 cup chopped fresh cilantro (optional)
- Lime wedges for serving

For the Pad Thai Sauce:

- 3 tablespoons soy sauce (or tamari for gluten-free)
- 2 tablespoons fish sauce (or vegetarian fish sauce)
- 2 tablespoons rice vinegar
- 1 tablespoon brown sugar (or coconut sugar)
- 1 tablespoon lime juice
- 1 teaspoon grated fresh ginger
- 1 teaspoon sriracha or chili sauce (adjust to taste)

Instructions:

- Preheat your oven to 400°F (200°C). Cut the spaghetti squash in half lengthwise and scoop out the seeds with a spoon. Place the squash halves, cut side down, on a baking sheet lined with parchment paper.

- Bake the spaghetti squash in the preheated oven for 30-40 minutes, or until the flesh is tender and can easily be pierced with a fork. Remove from the oven and let it cool slightly.

- While the spaghetti squash is baking, prepare the Pad Thai sauce. In a small bowl, whisk together the soy sauce, fish sauce, rice vinegar, brown sugar, lime juice, grated ginger, and sriracha until well combined. Set aside.

- Once the spaghetti squash has cooled enough to handle, use a fork to scrape the flesh into spaghetti-like strands. Set aside. Heat the olive oil in a large skillet or wok over medium-high heat. Add the minced garlic and thinly sliced onion, and cook for 2-3 minutes until softened and fragrant.

- Add the sliced red bell pepper, julienned carrot, and broccoli florets to the skillet. Cook for another 3-4 minutes, stirring occasionally, until the vegetables are tender-crisp. Push the vegetables to one side of the skillet, and pour the beaten eggs into the empty space. Cook, stirring gently, until the eggs are scrambled and cooked through.

- Add the cooked spaghetti squash noodles to the skillet, along with the prepared Pad Thai sauce. Toss everything together until well combined and heated through. Remove the skillet from the heat and stir in the chopped peanuts or cashews, thinly sliced green onions, and chopped fresh cilantro (if using).

66. Quinoa and Black Bean Salad

Ingredients:
- 1 cup quinoa, rinsed
- 2 cups water or vegetable broth
- 1 can (15 ounces) black beans, drained and rinsed
- 1 cup corn kernels (fresh, frozen, or canned)
- 1 red bell pepper, diced
- 1/2 red onion, finely chopped
- 1/4 cup chopped fresh cilantro
- Juice of 1 lime
- 2 tablespoons olive oil
- 1 teaspoon ground cumin
- 1/2 teaspoon chili powder
- Salt and pepper to taste
- Optional toppings: diced avocado, sliced green onions, crumbled feta cheese

Instructions:
- In a medium saucepan, bring the water or vegetable broth to a boil. Add the quinoa, reduce the heat to low, cover, and simmer for 15-20 minutes, or until the quinoa is cooked and the liquid is absorbed. Remove from heat and let it cool slightly.

- In a large mixing bowl, combine the cooked quinoa, black beans, corn kernels, diced red bell pepper, chopped red onion, and chopped cilantro.

- In a small bowl, whisk together the lime juice, olive oil, ground cumin, chili powder, salt, and pepper to make the dressing.

- Pour the dressing over the quinoa and black bean mixture, and toss until everything is well coated.

- Taste and adjust seasoning with additional salt, pepper, or lime juice, if needed.

- Cover the bowl and refrigerate the quinoa and black bean salad for at least 30 minutes to allow the flavors to meld.

- Before serving, give the salad a good stir and adjust seasoning if necessary.

- Serve the quinoa and black bean salad chilled, topped with optional toppings such as diced avocado, sliced green onions, or crumbled feta cheese.

This quinoa and black bean salad is not only delicious and satisfying but also packed with protein, fiber, and essential nutrients. It's a perfect dish for meal prep, picnics, potlucks, or as a side dish for any occasion. Enjoy this wholesome and flavorful salad!

67. Lemon Herb Tilapia

Lemon herb tilapia is a light, flavorful, and nutritious dish that's quick and easy to prepare, making it ideal for managing ADHD symptoms. Here's a recipe tailored for women with ADHD, emphasizing wholesome ingredients and simple preparation:

Ingredients:
- 4 tilapia fillets
- 2 tablespoons olive oil
- 2 cloves garlic, minced
- Zest and juice of 1 lemon
- 1 tablespoon chopped fresh parsley
- 1 tablespoon chopped fresh dill (or 1 teaspoon dried dill)
- Salt and pepper to taste
- Lemon wedges for serving

Instructions:
- Preheat your oven to 375°F (190°C). Line a baking sheet with parchment paper or lightly grease it with olive oil.

- Place the tilapia fillets on the prepared baking sheet in a single layer.

- In a small bowl, whisk together the olive oil, minced garlic, lemon zest, lemon juice, chopped parsley, chopped dill, salt, and pepper to make the marinade.

- Pour the marinade over the tilapia fillets, coating them evenly on both sides. Use a brush or your hands to spread the marinade evenly.

- Let the tilapia marinate for 10-15 minutes at room temperature to allow the flavors to meld.

- Transfer the baking sheet to the preheated oven and bake the tilapia for 12-15 minutes, or until the fish is cooked through and flakes easily with a fork.

- Remove the tilapia from the oven and let it rest for a few minutes before serving.

- Serve the lemon herb tilapia hot, garnished with lemon wedges for squeezing over the fish.

This lemon herb tilapia is not only delicious and flavorful but also rich in omega-3 fatty acids and protein. It pairs well with a variety of side dishes such as steamed vegetables, quinoa, or a fresh green salad. Enjoy this nutritious and satisfying dish!

68. Stir-Fried Tofu with Teriyaki Sauce

Ingredients:

- 1 block (14 ounces) firm tofu, drained and pressed
- 2 tablespoons soy sauce (or tamari for gluten-free)
- 2 tablespoons mirin (Japanese sweet rice wine)
- 1 tablespoon rice vinegar
- 1 tablespoon honey (or maple syrup for a vegan option)
- 1 tablespoon sesame oil
- 1 teaspoon grated fresh ginger
- 2 tablespoons cornstarch
- 2 tablespoons water
- 2 tablespoons vegetable oil (for frying)
- Optional vegetables: sliced bell peppers, broccoli florets, snap peas, carrots, or mushrooms
- Cooked rice or noodles for serving
- Sesame seeds and sliced green onions for garnish
- 2 cloves garlic, minced

Instructions:

- Cut the pressed tofu into cubes or rectangles, about 1/2 inch thick. In a small bowl, whisk together the soy sauce, mirin, rice vinegar, honey, sesame oil, minced garlic, and grated ginger to make the teriyaki sauce. Set aside.

- In another small bowl, mix together the cornstarch and water to make a slurry. Set aside. Heat the vegetable oil in a large skillet or wok over medium-high heat.

- Add the tofu cubes to the hot oil in a single layer, making sure not to overcrowd the pan. Fry the tofu for 3-4 minutes on each side, or until golden brown and crispy. Remove the tofu from the skillet and set aside on a plate lined with paper towels to drain excess oil.

- In the same skillet or wok, add the optional vegetables (if using) and stir-fry for 3-4 minutes, or until they are tender-crisp.

- Return the fried tofu to the skillet or wok with the vegetables, and pour the teriyaki sauce over the tofu and vegetables. Stir gently to coat everything evenly with the sauce.

- Add the cornstarch slurry to the skillet or wok, stirring continuously until the sauce thickens and coats the tofu and vegetables.

- Remove the skillet or wok from the heat and transfer the stir-fried tofu and vegetables to a serving dish. Serve the stir-fried tofu with teriyaki sauce hot, with cooked rice or noodles on the side. Garnish with sesame seeds and sliced green onions before serving.

This stir-fried tofu with teriyaki sauce is not only flavorful and satisfying but also rich in plant-based protein and nutrients. It's a versatile dish that can be customized with your favorite vegetables and served as a quick and easy weeknight meal. Enjoy this delicious and wholesome recipe!

69. Greek Chicken Salad

Ingredients:
- 2 boneless, skinless chicken breasts
- 2 tablespoons olive oil
- 1 teaspoon dried oregano
- 1/2 teaspoon dried thyme
- Salt and pepper to taste
- 4 cups mixed salad greens
(such as romaine, spinach, and arugula)
- 1 cup cherry tomatoes, halved
- 1/2 cucumber, sliced
- 1/4 red onion, thinly sliced
- 1/4 cup crumbled feta cheese
- Optional toppings: sliced bell peppers, sliced red radishes, pepperoncini peppers
- For the Greek Salad Dressing:
- 1/4 cup extra virgin olive oil
- 2 tablespoons red wine vinegar
- 1 clove garlic, minced
- 1 teaspoon dried oregano
- Salt and pepper to taste
- 1/2 cup pitted Kalamata olives

Instructions:
- Preheat your oven to 375°F (190°C).

- Place the chicken breasts on a baking sheet lined with parchment paper or aluminum foil. Drizzle the chicken breasts with olive oil and sprinkle them with dried oregano, dried thyme, salt, and pepper, rubbing the seasoning into the chicken.

- Bake the chicken breasts in the preheated oven for 25-30 minutes, or until they are cooked through and no longer pink in the center. Remove from the oven and let them cool slightly before slicing.

- While the chicken is baking, prepare the Greek salad dressing. In a small bowl, whisk together the extra virgin olive oil, red wine vinegar, minced garlic, dried oregano, salt, and pepper until well combined. Set aside.

- In a large mixing bowl, combine the mixed salad greens, halved cherry tomatoes, sliced cucumber, thinly sliced red onion, pitted Kalamata olives, and crumbled feta cheese.

- Once the chicken breasts have cooled slightly, slice them into thin strips. Add the sliced chicken to the salad bowl.

- Drizzle the Greek salad dressing over the salad ingredients in the bowl, tossing gently to coat everything evenly with the dressing. Divide the Greek chicken salad among serving plates or bowls.

- Garnish with optional toppings such as sliced bell peppers, sliced red radishes, or pepperoncini peppers, if desired. Serve the Greek chicken salad immediately, and enjoy!

70. Lentil and Vegetable Curry

Ingredients:
- 1 cup dried lentils (brown or green), rinsed and drained
- 2 cups vegetable broth
- 1 tablespoon olive oil
- 1 onion, diced
- 2 cloves garlic, minced
- 1 tablespoon grated fresh ginger
- 1 tablespoon curry powder
- 1 teaspoon ground cumin
- 1 teaspoon ground coriander
- 1/2 teaspoon turmeric
- 1/4 teaspoon cayenne pepper (optional, for added heat)
- 1 can (14 ounces) diced tomatoes
- 1 can (14 ounces) coconut milk
- 2 cups chopped vegetables (such as carrots, bell peppers, zucchini, cauliflower, or spinach)
- Salt and pepper to taste
- Fresh cilantro leaves for garnish
- Cooked rice or naan bread for serving

Instructions:
- In a large pot or Dutch oven, heat the olive oil over medium heat. Add the diced onion and cook until softened, about 5 minutes.

- Add the minced garlic and grated ginger to the pot, and cook for another 1-2 minutes until fragrant.

- Stir in the curry powder, ground cumin, ground coriander, turmeric, and cayenne pepper (if using). Cook for 1 minute, stirring constantly, until the spices are toasted and fragrant.

- Add the rinsed lentils, vegetable broth, diced tomatoes (with their juices), and coconut milk to the pot. Stir to combine.

- Bring the mixture to a boil, then reduce the heat to low and simmer, covered, for 20-25 minutes, or until the lentils are tender and cooked through.

- Stir in the chopped vegetables of your choice. Simmer for an additional 10-15 minutes, or until the vegetables are tender.

- Season the lentil and vegetable curry with salt and pepper to taste. Adjust the seasoning and consistency as needed by adding more broth or coconut milk if it's too thick. Serve the lentil and vegetable curry hot, garnished with fresh cilantro leaves, and accompanied by cooked rice or naan bread.

This lentil and vegetable curry is not only delicious and satisfying but also packed with plant-based protein, fiber, and essential nutrients. It's a comforting and nourishing meal that's perfect for busy weeknights or meal prep. Enjoy this flavorful and nutritious recipe!

71. Grilled Vegetable Pasta Salad

Ingredients:

- 1/4 cup chopped fresh parsley
- Salt and pepper to taste
- Optional: grated Parmesan cheese for serving
- For the Balsamic Vinaigrette:
- 1/4 cup balsamic vinegar
- 2 tablespoons olive oil
- 1 teaspoon Dijon mustard
- 1 clove garlic, minced
- Salt and pepper to taste
- 8 ounces (about 225g) pasta of your choice (such as penne, fusilli, or rotini)
- 2 tablespoons olive oil
- 1 red bell pepper, sliced
- 1 yellow bell pepper, sliced
- 1 zucchini, sliced lengthwise into thin strips
- 1 yellow squash, sliced lengthwise into thin strips
- 1 small red onion, sliced into rounds
- 1 cup cherry tomatoes
- 1/4 cup chopped fresh basil

Instructions:

- Cook the pasta according to the package instructions until al dente. Drain and rinse under cold water to stop the cooking process. Set aside.

- Preheat your grill or grill pan to medium-high heat. In a large bowl, toss the sliced bell peppers, zucchini, yellow squash, and red onion with olive oil until evenly coated. Season with salt and pepper to taste.

- Grill the vegetables in batches, turning occasionally, until they are tender and lightly charred, about 3-4 minutes per side. Remove from the grill and let them cool slightly.

- In a small bowl, whisk together the balsamic vinegar, olive oil, Dijon mustard, minced garlic, salt, and pepper to make the balsamic vinaigrette.

- In a large mixing bowl, combine the cooked pasta, grilled vegetables, cherry tomatoes, chopped fresh basil, and chopped fresh parsley.

- Pour the balsamic vinaigrette over the pasta and vegetables, and toss gently to coat everything evenly with the dressing.

- Taste and adjust seasoning with additional salt and pepper, if needed. Serve the grilled vegetable pasta salad at room temperature or chilled, garnished with grated Parmesan cheese if desired.

This grilled vegetable pasta salad is not only delicious and satisfying but also packed with fiber, vitamins, and minerals. It's a versatile dish that can be served as a main meal or as a side dish for picnics, barbecues, or potlucks. Enjoy this flavorful and nutritious recipe!

72. Caprese Stuffed Chicken Breast

Ingredients:
- 4 boneless, skinless chicken breasts
- Salt and pepper to taste
- 2 tablespoons olive oil
- 2 medium tomatoes, thinly sliced
- 1/4 cup fresh basil leaves
- Balsamic glaze, for drizzling (optional)
- 4 slices fresh mozzarella cheese
- Toothpicks or kitchen twine, for securing

Instructions:
- Preheat your oven to 400°F (200°C).

- Place each chicken breast between two sheets of plastic wrap or wax paper. Using a meat mallet or rolling pin, gently pound the chicken breasts to an even thickness, about 1/2 inch thick.

- Season both sides of each chicken breast with salt and pepper to taste. Lay a slice of fresh mozzarella cheese on top of each chicken breast.

- Top the mozzarella cheese with a few slices of tomato and a couple of fresh basil leaves.

- Roll up each chicken breast tightly, starting from the narrow end, to enclose the filling. Secure with toothpicks or kitchen twine to hold the rolls together.

- Heat the olive oil in an oven-safe skillet over medium-high heat. Once hot, add the stuffed chicken breasts to the skillet and sear them for 2-3 minutes on each side, or until golden brown.

- Transfer the skillet to the preheated oven and bake the stuffed chicken breasts for 20-25 minutes, or until the chicken is cooked through and reaches an internal temperature of 165°F (75°C).

- Remove the stuffed chicken breasts from the oven and let them rest for a few minutes before serving.

- To serve, remove the toothpicks or kitchen twine from the chicken breasts and slice them into rounds. Drizzle with balsamic glaze, if desired, and garnish with additional fresh basil leaves. Serve the Caprese stuffed chicken breasts hot, alongside your favorite side dishes.

This Caprese stuffed chicken breast is not only delicious and satisfying but also a beautiful and elegant dish that's perfect for special occasions or weeknight dinners. Enjoy the combination of juicy chicken, melty mozzarella, ripe tomatoes, and fragrant basil in every bite!

73. Moroccan Chickpea Stew

Ingredients:

- 2 tablespoons olive oil
- 1 onion, diced
- 3 cloves garlic, minced
- 1 teaspoon ground cumin
- 1 teaspoon ground coriander
- 1 teaspoon ground turmeric
- 1/2 teaspoon ground cinnamon
- 1/4 teaspoon ground ginger
- Pinch of cayenne pepper (optional, for added heat)
- 1 can (14 ounces) diced tomatoes
- 1 can (14 ounces) chickpeas, drained and rinsed
- 2 cups vegetable broth
- 1 cup diced carrots
- 1 cup diced sweet potatoes
- 1 cup diced bell peppers (any color)
- 1/2 cup dried apricots, chopped
- Salt and pepper to taste
- Fresh cilantro or parsley for garnish
- Cooked couscous or rice for serving

Instructions:

- In a large pot or Dutch oven, heat the olive oil over medium heat.

- Add the diced onion to the pot and cook until softened, about 5 minutes.

- Add the minced garlic, ground cumin, ground coriander, ground turmeric, ground cinnamon, ground ginger, and cayenne pepper (if using) to the pot. Cook for 1-2 minutes, stirring constantly, until the spices are fragrant.

- Stir in the diced tomatoes, chickpeas, vegetable broth, diced carrots, diced sweet potatoes, diced bell peppers, and chopped dried apricots.

- Bring the mixture to a boil, then reduce the heat to low and simmer, covered, for 20-25 minutes, or until the vegetables are tender.

- Season the Moroccan chickpea stew with salt and pepper to taste. Adjust the seasoning and consistency as needed by adding more broth or water if it's too thick.

- Serve the Moroccan chickpea stew hot, garnished with fresh cilantro or parsley, and accompanied by cooked couscous or rice.

This Moroccan chickpea stew is not only delicious and satisfying but also packed with fiber, protein, and essential nutrients. It's a comforting and nourishing meal that's perfect for cold weather or anytime you're craving a flavorful and hearty dish. Enjoy this flavorful and nutritious recipe!

74. Turkey and Cranberry Stuffed Acorn Squash

- **Ingredients:**
- 2 acorn squash
- 1 tablespoon olive oil
- Salt and pepper to taste
- 1 pound ground turkey
- 1 small onion, diced
- 2 cloves garlic, minced
- 1/2 cup dried cranberries
- 1 teaspoon dried sage
- 1/2 teaspoon dried thyme
- 1/2 teaspoon dried rosemary
- 1/4 teaspoon ground cinnamon
- 1/4 cup grated Parmesan cheese (optional)
- Fresh parsley for garnish
- 1/4 cup chopped pecans or walnuts (optional)

Instructions:

- Preheat your oven to 400Â°F (200Â°C). Cut the acorn squash in half lengthwise and scoop out the seeds with a spoon. Brush the cut sides of the squash halves with olive oil and sprinkle with salt and pepper.

- Place the squash halves, cut side down, on a baking sheet lined with parchment paper. Roast in the preheated oven for 25-30 minutes, or until the squash is tender when pierced with a fork.

- While the squash is roasting, heat the olive oil in a large skillet over medium heat. Add the diced onion and minced garlic, and cook until softened, about 5 minutes.

- Add the ground turkey to the skillet and cook until browned and cooked through, breaking it up with a spoon as it cooks.

- Stir in the dried cranberries, chopped pecans or walnuts (if using), dried sage, dried thyme, dried rosemary, and ground cinnamon. Cook for another 2-3 minutes to allow the flavors to meld.

- Once the acorn squash halves are done roasting, remove them from the oven and flip them over so the cut sides are facing up.

- Fill each squash half with the turkey and cranberry mixture, pressing down gently to pack it in. Sprinkle the stuffed squash halves with grated Parmesan cheese (if using).

- Return the stuffed squash to the oven and bake for an additional 10-15 minutes, or until the filling is heated through and the cheese is melted and bubbly. Remove the stuffed squash from the oven and garnish with fresh parsley before serving.

This turkey and cranberry stuffed acorn squash is not only delicious and satisfying but also packed with protein, fiber, and essential nutrients. It's a comforting and festive dish that's perfect for holiday gatherings or cozy family dinners.

75. Tofu Lettuce Wraps

Ingredients:
- 1 block (14 ounces) firm tofu
- 2 tablespoons olive oil
- 2 cloves garlic, minced
- 1 small onion, finely chopped
- 1 red bell pepper, diced
- 1 carrot, grated
- 1/2 cup water chestnuts, chopped
- 2 tablespoons soy sauce
(or tamari for gluten-free)
- 1 tablespoon hoisin sauce
- 1 tablespoon rice vinegar
- 1 teaspoon sesame oil
- 1 teaspoon grated fresh ginger
- 1 tablespoon chopped green onions (for garnish)
- 1 tablespoon chopped fresh cilantro (for garnish)
- 1 head iceberg or butter lettuce, leaves separated

Instructions:
- Press the tofu to remove excess moisture. Cut the tofu into small cubes and set aside. Heat the olive oil in a large skillet or wok over medium heat.

- Add the minced garlic and finely chopped onion to the skillet. Cook for 2-3 minutes, or until the onion is translucent and fragrant.

- Add the diced red bell pepper, grated carrot, and chopped water chestnuts to the skillet. Cook for another 3-4 minutes, or until the vegetables are tender-crisp.

- Push the vegetables to one side of the skillet and add the tofu cubes to the empty space. Cook the tofu for 4-5 minutes, stirring occasionally, until golden brown.

- In a small bowl, whisk together the soy sauce, hoisin sauce, rice vinegar, sesame oil, and grated fresh ginger to make the sauce.

- Pour the sauce over the tofu and vegetables in the skillet. Stir to coat everything evenly with the sauce. Cook for another 2-3 minutes, or until the sauce is heated through and the tofu and vegetables are coated and glazed.

- Remove the skillet from the heat and sprinkle the chopped green onions and fresh cilantro over the tofu mixture.

- To serve, spoon the tofu mixture into the lettuce leaves, using them as wraps or cups. Garnish with additional chopped green onions and fresh cilantro, if desired. Serve the tofu lettuce wraps immediately, and enjoy!

These tofu lettuce wraps are not only delicious and satisfying but also packed with protein, fiber, and essential nutrients. They make a perfect light and flavorful meal for lunch or dinner, and they're also great for entertaining. Enjoy this wholesome and flavorful recipe!

76. Roasted Cauliflower with Tahini Sauce

Ingredients:
- 1 head cauliflower, cut into florets
- 2 tablespoons olive oil
- Salt and pepper to taste
- 2 tablespoons tahini
- 2 tablespoons lemon juice
- 1 clove garlic, minced
- 2-3 tablespoons water
- Optional toppings: chopped fresh parsley, toasted sesame seeds, red pepper flakes

Instructions:
- Preheat your oven to 425°F (220°C).

- Place the cauliflower florets on a baking sheet lined with parchment paper.

- Drizzle the cauliflower florets with olive oil and season with salt and pepper to taste. Toss to coat evenly.

- Roast the cauliflower in the preheated oven for 25-30 minutes, or until golden brown and tender, stirring halfway through cooking.

- While the cauliflower is roasting, prepare the tahini sauce. In a small bowl, whisk together the tahini, lemon juice, minced garlic, and water until smooth and creamy. Add more water as needed to achieve your desired consistency.

- Once the cauliflower is done roasting, transfer it to a serving platter or plate.

- Drizzle the tahini sauce over the roasted cauliflower.

- Garnish with chopped fresh parsley, toasted sesame seeds, and red pepper flakes, if desired.

- Serve the roasted cauliflower with tahini sauce immediately, and enjoy!

This roasted cauliflower with tahini sauce is not only delicious and satisfying but also packed with fiber, vitamins, and minerals. It makes a perfect side dish for any meal or a healthy snack on its own. Enjoy this wholesome and flavorful recipe!

77. Greek Quinoa Salad

Ingredients:

- 1 cup quinoa, rinsed
- 2 cups water or vegetable broth
- 1 cucumber, diced
- 1 bell pepper (any color), diced
- 1 pint cherry tomatoes, halved
- 1/2 red onion, finely chopped
- 1/2 cup pitted Kalamata olives, halved
- 1/2 cup crumbled feta cheese
- 1/4 cup chopped fresh parsley
- 1/4 cup chopped fresh mint
- Juice of 1 lemon
- 2 tablespoons extra virgin olive oil
- 1 teaspoon dried oregano
- Salt and pepper to taste

Instructions:

- In a medium saucepan, bring the water or vegetable broth to a boil. Add the quinoa, reduce the heat to low, cover, and simmer for 15-20 minutes, or until the quinoa is cooked and the liquid is absorbed. Remove from heat and let it cool slightly.

- In a large mixing bowl, combine the cooked quinoa, diced cucumber, diced bell pepper, halved cherry tomatoes, finely chopped red onion, halved Kalamata olives, crumbled feta cheese, chopped fresh parsley, and chopped fresh mint.

- In a small bowl, whisk together the lemon juice, extra virgin olive oil, dried oregano, salt, and pepper to make the dressing.

- Pour the dressing over the quinoa salad and toss until everything is well coated. Taste and adjust seasoning with additional salt, pepper, or lemon juice, if needed.

- Cover the bowl and refrigerate the Greek quinoa salad for at least 30 minutes to allow the flavors to meld.

- Before serving, give the salad a good stir and adjust seasoning if necessary. Serve the Greek quinoa salad chilled, as a side dish or a light meal on its own.

This Greek quinoa salad is not only delicious and satisfying but also packed with protein, fiber, and essential nutrients. It's a perfect dish for meal prep, picnics, potlucks, or as a side dish for any occasion. Enjoy this wholesome and flavorful recipe!

78. Lemon Garlic Shrimp and Asparagus

Ingredients:
- 1 pound large shrimp, peeled and deveined
- 1 bunch asparagus, trimmed and cut into bite-sized pieces
- 3 tablespoons olive oil, divided
- 4 cloves garlic, minced
- Zest and juice of 1 lemon
- Salt and pepper to taste
- 1/4 teaspoon red pepper flakes (optional)
- Chopped fresh parsley for garnish

Instructions:

- Preheat your oven to 400Â°F (200Â°C).

- Place the shrimp and asparagus on a large baking sheet lined with parchment paper.

- Drizzle 2 tablespoons of olive oil over the shrimp and asparagus. Add the minced garlic, lemon zest, lemon juice, salt, pepper, and red pepper flakes (if using). Toss everything together until well coated.

- Arrange the shrimp and asparagus in a single layer on the baking sheet.

- Roast in the preheated oven for 10-12 minutes, or until the shrimp are pink and opaque and the asparagus is tender-crisp.

- Remove from the oven and drizzle with the remaining tablespoon of olive oil.

- Garnish with chopped fresh parsley before serving.

- Serve the lemon garlic shrimp and asparagus hot, alongside cooked rice, quinoa, or crusty bread.

This lemon garlic shrimp and asparagus dish is not only delicious and satisfying but also packed with protein, fiber, and essential nutrients. It's a quick and easy meal that's perfect for busy weeknights or as a light and flavorful option for any occasion. Enjoy this wholesome and flavorful recipe!

79. Chicken and Vegetable Skillet

Ingredients:

- 2 cups broccoli florets
- 1 cup cherry tomatoes, halved
- 2 tablespoons soy sauce
(or tamari for gluten-free)
- 1 tablespoon honey
(or maple syrup for a vegan option)
- 1 tablespoon rice vinegar
- Cooked rice or quinoa for serving
- Fresh parsley or cilantro for garnish
- 1 pound boneless, skinless chicken breasts, cut into bite-sized pieces
- 2 tablespoons olive oil, divided
- 1 teaspoon garlic powder
- 1 teaspoon paprika
- Salt and pepper to taste
- 1 onion, diced
- 2 bell peppers (any color), diced
- 2 cups sliced mushrooms
- 2 cloves garlic, minced

Instructions:

- In a large bowl, toss the chicken pieces with 1 tablespoon of olive oil, garlic powder, paprika, salt, and pepper until evenly coated. Heat the remaining tablespoon of olive oil in a large skillet over medium-high heat.

- Add the seasoned chicken to the skillet and cook for 5-6 minutes, or until browned and cooked through. Remove the chicken from the skillet and set aside.

- In the same skillet, add the diced onion and bell peppers. Cook for 3-4 minutes, or until softened.

- Add the sliced mushrooms, broccoli florets, cherry tomatoes, and minced garlic to the skillet. Cook for another 4-5 minutes, or until the vegetables are tender-crisp.

- In a small bowl, whisk together the soy sauce, honey, and rice vinegar to make the sauce.

- Return the cooked chicken to the skillet and pour the sauce over the chicken and vegetables. Stir to coat everything evenly with the sauce.

- Cook for another 2-3 minutes, or until the sauce is heated through and the chicken and vegetables are coated and glazed.

- Remove the skillet from the heat and serve the chicken and vegetable mixture hot, alongside cooked rice or quinoa. Garnish with fresh parsley or cilantro, if desired.

This chicken and vegetable skillet is not only delicious and satisfying but also packed with protein, fiber, and essential nutrients. It's a versatile dish that's perfect for a quick and easy weeknight meal. Enjoy this wholesome and flavorful recipe!

80. Spinach and Ricotta Stuffed Shells

Ingredients:
- 1 box (12 ounces) jumbo pasta shells
- 2 cups ricotta cheese
- 1 cup shredded mozzarella cheese, divided
- 1/2 cup grated Parmesan cheese, divided
- 1 egg, lightly beaten
- 2 cups fresh spinach, chopped
- 2 cloves garlic, minced
- 1 teaspoon dried basil
- 1 teaspoon dried oregano
- Salt and pepper to taste
- 1 jar (24 ounces) marinara sauce
- Fresh basil leaves for garnish (optional)

Instructions:
- Preheat your oven to 375Â°F (190Â°C).

- Cook the jumbo pasta shells according to the package instructions until al dente. Drain and rinse under cold water to stop the cooking process. Set aside.

- In a large mixing bowl, combine the ricotta cheese, 1/2 cup shredded mozzarella cheese, 1/4 cup grated Parmesan cheese, beaten egg, chopped spinach, minced garlic, dried basil, dried oregano, salt, and pepper. Mix until well combined.

- Spread a thin layer of marinara sauce on the bottom of a 9x13-inch baking dish.

- Stuff each cooked pasta shell with the spinach and ricotta mixture and place them in the baking dish.

- Pour the remaining marinara sauce over the stuffed shells, covering them evenly.

- Sprinkle the remaining shredded mozzarella cheese and grated Parmesan cheese over the top of the stuffed shells.

- Cover the baking dish with aluminum foil and bake in the preheated oven for 25-30 minutes, or until the cheese is melted and bubbly.

- Remove the foil and bake for an additional 5-10 minutes, or until the cheese is golden brown.

- Remove from the oven and let it cool for a few minutes before serving. Garnish with fresh basil leaves, if desired. Serve the spinach and ricotta stuffed shells hot, and enjoy!

These spinach and ricotta stuffed shells are not only delicious and satisfying but also packed with protein, calcium, and essential nutrients. They make a perfect comforting meal for dinner or a special occasion. Enjoy this wholesome and flavorful recipe!

81. Veggie Sushi Rolls

Ingredients:

- 2 cups sushi rice
- 4 nori seaweed sheets
- 1 cucumber, julienned
- 1 carrot, julienned
- 1 avocado, sliced
- 1 bell pepper (any color), thinly sliced
- 1/2 cup sliced mushrooms (such as shiitake or cremini)
- Pickled ginger, for serving (optional)
- Wasabi, for serving (optional)
- Soy sauce or tamari, for serving (optional)

Instructions:

- Rinse the sushi rice in a fine mesh strainer under cold water until the water runs clear. Cook the rice according to the package instructions, using slightly less water than usual for a firmer texture. Once cooked, let it cool slightly.

- Place a nori seaweed sheet shiny side down on a bamboo sushi rolling mat or a clean kitchen towel.

- Spread a thin layer of sushi rice evenly over the nori sheet, leaving about a half-inch border at the top edge.

- Arrange the julienned cucumber, carrot, avocado slices, bell pepper slices, and sliced mushrooms in a row along the bottom edge of the rice-covered nori sheet.

- Starting from the bottom edge, tightly roll the nori sheet and rice over the filling, using the bamboo sushi rolling mat or kitchen towel to help shape and compress the roll.

- Continue rolling until you reach the top edge, sealing the edge with a little water if necessary.

- Repeat the process with the remaining nori sheets and filling ingredients.

- Once all the rolls are assembled, use a sharp knife to slice each roll into 6-8 pieces.

- Serve the veggie sushi rolls with pickled ginger, wasabi, and soy sauce or tamari on the side, if desired.

These veggie sushi rolls are not only delicious and satisfying but also packed with fiber, vitamins, and minerals. They make a perfect light and nutritious meal or snack, and they're also great for meal prep or entertaining. Enjoy making and eating these flavorful and nutritious veggie sushi rolls!

82. Mediterranean Stuffed Peppers

Ingredients:

- 1/2 cup sliced Kalamata olives
- 1/2 cup crumbled feta cheese
- 1/4 cup chopped fresh parsley
- 1/4 cup chopped fresh basil
- 1 teaspoon dried oregano
- Salt and pepper to taste
- Optional: Lemon wedges for serving
- 4 large bell peppers (any color), halved and seeds removed
- 1 cup quinoa, rinsed
- 2 cups vegetable broth or water
- 1 tablespoon olive oil
- 1 small onion, diced
- 2 cloves garlic, minced
- 1 cup diced tomatoes (fresh or canned)

Instructions:

- Preheat your oven to 375°F (190°C).

- In a medium saucepan, bring the vegetable broth or water to a boil. Add the quinoa, reduce the heat to low, cover, and simmer for 15-20 minutes, or until the quinoa is cooked and the liquid is absorbed. Remove from heat and let it cool slightly.

- In a large skillet, heat the olive oil over medium heat. Add the diced onion and minced garlic, and cook for 2-3 minutes, or until softened.

- Add the diced tomatoes to the skillet and cook for another 3-4 minutes, or until slightly softened.

- Stir in the cooked quinoa, sliced Kalamata olives, crumbled feta cheese, chopped fresh parsley, chopped fresh basil, and dried oregano. Season with salt and pepper to taste. Cook for another 2-3 minutes to allow the flavors to meld.

- Arrange the halved bell peppers in a baking dish, cut side up. Spoon the quinoa mixture into each bell pepper half, pressing down gently to pack it in. Cover the baking dish with aluminum foil and bake in the preheated oven for 30-35 minutes, or until the peppers are tender.

- Remove the foil and bake for an additional 5-10 minutes, or until the filling is heated through and the tops of the peppers are lightly browned.

- Remove from the oven and let the stuffed peppers cool for a few minutes before serving. Serve the Mediterranean stuffed peppers hot, garnished with additional chopped fresh parsley or basil and lemon wedges on the side, if desired.

These Mediterranean stuffed peppers are not only delicious and satisfying but also packed with protein, fiber, and essential nutrients. They make a perfect light and flavorful meal for lunch or dinner, and they're also great for meal prep or entertaining.

83. Baked Salmon with Dill Sauce

Ingredients:

- 4 salmon fillets
- Salt and pepper to taste
- 2 tablespoons olive oil
- 1 tablespoon lemon juice
- 2 tablespoons chopped fresh dill
- For the Dill Sauce:
- 1/2 cup Greek yogurt
- 2 tablespoons chopped fresh dill
- 1 tablespoon lemon juice
- 1 clove garlic, minced
- Salt and pepper to taste

Instructions:

- Preheat your oven to 400Â°F (200Â°C).

- Place the salmon fillets on a baking sheet lined with parchment paper. Season with salt and pepper to taste.

- In a small bowl, whisk together the olive oil and lemon juice. Brush the mixture over the salmon fillets.

- Sprinkle the chopped fresh dill over the salmon.

- Bake the salmon in the preheated oven for 12-15 minutes, or until the salmon is cooked through and flakes easily with a fork.

- While the salmon is baking, prepare the dill sauce. In a small bowl, mix together the Greek yogurt, chopped fresh dill, lemon juice, minced garlic, salt, and pepper.

- Serve the baked salmon hot, with the dill sauce drizzled on top or served on the side.

This baked salmon with dill sauce is not only delicious and satisfying but also packed with protein, omega-3 fatty acids, and essential nutrients. It's a quick and easy meal that's perfect for busy weeknights or as a special dish for entertaining. Enjoy this wholesome and flavorful recipe!

84. Quinoa and Vegetable Stir-Fry

Ingredients:
- 1 cup quinoa, rinsed
- 2 cups water or vegetable broth
- 2 tablespoons olive oil
- 2 cloves garlic, minced
- 1 small onion, thinly sliced
- 1 bell pepper (any color), thinly sliced
- 2 carrots, thinly sliced
- 1 cup broccoli florets
- 1 cup snap peas, trimmed
- 1 cup sliced mushrooms
- 1/4 cup soy sauce or tamari
- 2 tablespoons rice vinegar
- 1 tablespoon honey or maple syrup
- 1 teaspoon grated fresh ginger
- Sesame seeds for garnish (optional)
- Chopped green onions for garnish (optional)

Instructions:
- In a medium saucepan, combine the quinoa and water or vegetable broth. Bring to a boil, then reduce the heat to low, cover, and simmer for 15-20 minutes, or until the quinoa is cooked and the liquid is absorbed. Remove from heat and let it sit, covered, for 5 minutes. Fluff with a fork and set aside.

- In a large skillet or wok, heat the olive oil over medium-high heat.

- Add the minced garlic and thinly sliced onion to the skillet. Cook for 2-3 minutes, or until the onion is translucent and fragrant.

- Add the thinly sliced bell pepper, carrots, broccoli florets, snap peas, and sliced mushrooms to the skillet. Cook for another 5-6 minutes, or until the vegetables are tender-crisp.

- In a small bowl, whisk together the soy sauce or tamari, rice vinegar, honey or maple syrup, and grated fresh ginger to make the sauce.

- Pour the sauce over the cooked vegetables in the skillet. Stir to coat everything evenly with the sauce.

- Add the cooked quinoa to the skillet. Stir to combine with the vegetables and sauce. Cook for another 2-3 minutes, or until everything is heated through.

- Remove from heat and garnish with sesame seeds and chopped green onions, if desired. Serve the quinoa and vegetable stir-fry hot, and enjoy!

This quinoa and vegetable stir-fry is not only delicious and satisfying but also packed with protein, fiber, vitamins, and minerals. It's a versatile dish that's perfect for a quick and easy weeknight meal. Enjoy this wholesome and flavorful recipe!

85. Greek Turkey Burgers with Tzatziki Sauce

Ingredients:

For the Turkey Burgers:

- 1 pound ground turkey
- 1/4 cup finely chopped red onion
- 2 cloves garlic, minced
- 1/4 cup chopped fresh parsley
- 1 tablespoon chopped fresh oregano
(or 1 teaspoon dried oregano)
- 1 teaspoon ground cumin
- 1 teaspoon paprika
- Salt and pepper to taste
- Olive oil for cooking
- Burger buns or lettuce wraps, for serving
- Optional toppings: sliced tomatoes, cucumber, red onion, lettuce

For the Tzatziki Sauce:

- 1 cup Greek yogurt
- 1/2 cucumber, grated and squeezed to remove excess moisture
- 1 clove garlic, minced
- 1 tablespoon chopped fresh dill
- 1 tablespoon lemon juice
- Salt and pepper to taste

Instructions:

For the Turkey Burgers:

- In a large mixing bowl, combine the ground turkey, finely chopped red onion, minced garlic, chopped fresh parsley, chopped fresh oregano, ground cumin, paprika, salt, and pepper. Mix until well combined.
- Divide the turkey mixture into 4 equal portions and shape each portion into a burger patty.
- Heat a grill pan or skillet over medium heat and lightly brush with olive oil.
- Cook the turkey burgers for 4-5 minutes on each side, or until cooked through and browned on the outside. Remove from heat and let the burgers rest for a few minutes.

For the Tzatziki Sauce:

- In a small bowl, combine the Greek yogurt, grated cucumber, minced garlic, chopped fresh dill, lemon juice, salt, and pepper. Mix until well combined.
- Taste and adjust seasoning, adding more salt, pepper, or lemon juice if desired.
- Assembling the Burgers:
- Serve the cooked turkey burgers on burger buns or lettuce wraps.
- Top each burger with a dollop of tzatziki sauce.
- Add optional toppings such as sliced tomatoes, cucumber, red onion, and lettuce.
- Serve immediately, and enjoy!

These Greek turkey burgers with tzatziki sauce are not only delicious and satisfying but also packed with protein, vitamins, and minerals. They make a perfect meal for lunch or dinner, and they're also great for meal prep or outdoor grilling. Enjoy this wholesome and flavorful recipe!

86. Eggplant Rollatini

Ingredients:
For the Eggplant:
- 2 large eggplants, sliced lengthwise into 1/4-inch thick slices
- Salt
- Olive oil for brushing

For the Filling:
- 1 cup ricotta cheese
- 1/2 cup grated Parmesan cheese
- 1 egg, lightly beaten
- 2 cloves garlic, minced
- 1/4 cup chopped fresh basil
- Salt and pepper to taste
- For the Tomato Sauce:
- 2 cups tomato sauce (homemade or store-bought)
- 1 teaspoon dried oregano
- 1 teaspoon dried basil
- Salt and pepper to taste

For Assembly:
- 1 cup shredded mozzarella cheese
- Fresh basil leaves for garnish (optional)

Instructions:
Preparing the Eggplant:
- Lay the eggplant slices on a baking sheet lined with paper towels. Sprinkle both sides of the slices generously with salt and let them sit for about 30 minutes. This helps draw out excess moisture and bitterness from the eggplant.

- After 30 minutes, pat the eggplant slices dry with paper towels to remove the excess moisture.

- Preheat your oven to 400°F (200°C). Brush both sides of the eggplant slices with olive oil and place them on a baking sheet lined with parchment paper.

- Roast the eggplant slices in the preheated oven for 15-20 minutes, or until they are tender and lightly browned. Remove from the oven and set aside.

Making the Filling:
In a mixing bowl, combine the ricotta cheese, grated Parmesan cheese, lightly beaten egg, minced garlic, chopped fresh basil, salt, and pepper. Mix until well combined.

Making the Tomato Sauce:
In a saucepan, heat the tomato sauce over medium heat. Add the dried oregano, dried basil, salt, and pepper. Stir to combine and let the sauce simmer for 5-10 minutes.

Assembling the Rollatini:
- Spread a thin layer of tomato sauce on the bottom of a baking dish.

- Take an eggplant slice and place a spoonful of the ricotta filling at one end. Roll up the eggplant slice and place it seam-side down in the baking dish.

- Repeat with the remaining eggplant slices and ricotta filling.

- Once all the eggplant slices are rolled and placed in the baking dish, spoon the remaining tomato sauce over the top.

- Sprinkle the shredded mozzarella cheese over the tomato sauce.

- Cover the baking dish with aluminum foil and bake in the preheated oven for 20-25 minutes, or until the cheese is melted and bubbly.

- Remove the foil and bake for an additional 5-10 minutes, or until the cheese is golden brown.

- Remove from the oven and let the eggplant rollatini cool for a few minutes before serving.

- Garnish with fresh basil leaves, if desired.

This eggplant rollatini is not only delicious and satisfying but also packed with fiber, vitamins, and minerals. It makes a perfect comforting meal for dinner or a special occasion. Enjoy this wholesome and flavorful recipe!

87. Teriyaki Vegetable Stir-Fry

Ingredients:

- 1 cup sliced mushrooms
- 1/4 cup soy sauce or tamari
- 2 tablespoons rice vinegar
- 1 tablespoon honey or maple syrup
- 1 teaspoon grated fresh ginger
- 1 tablespoon cornstarch (optional, for thickening)
- Sesame seeds for garnish (optional)
- Chopped green onions for garnish (optional)
- 1 cup quinoa or rice, cooked according to package instructions
- 2 tablespoons olive oil
- 2 cloves garlic, minced
- 1 small onion, thinly sliced
- 1 bell pepper (any color), thinly sliced
- 2 carrots, thinly sliced
- 1 cup broccoli florets
- 1 cup snap peas, trimmed

Instructions:

- In a large skillet or wok, heat the olive oil over medium-high heat.

- Add the minced garlic and thinly sliced onion to the skillet. Cook for 2-3 minutes, or until the onion is translucent and fragrant.

- Add the thinly sliced bell pepper, carrots, broccoli florets, snap peas, and sliced mushrooms to the skillet. Cook for another 5-6 minutes, or until the vegetables are tender-crisp.

- In a small bowl, whisk together the soy sauce or tamari, rice vinegar, honey or maple syrup, and grated fresh ginger to make the teriyaki sauce.

- If using cornstarch, dissolve it in 2 tablespoons of water, then add it to the teriyaki sauce and whisk to combine.

- Pour the teriyaki sauce over the cooked vegetables in the skillet. Stir to coat everything evenly with the sauce.

- Cook for another 2-3 minutes, or until the sauce has thickened slightly and everything is heated through.

- Remove from heat and serve the teriyaki vegetable stir-fry over cooked quinoa or rice.

- Garnish with sesame seeds and chopped green onions, if desired.

This teriyaki vegetable stir-fry is not only delicious and satisfying but also packed with fiber, vitamins, and minerals. It's a versatile dish that's perfect for a quick and easy weeknight meal. Enjoy this wholesome and flavorful recipe!

88. Shrimp and Avocado Salad

Ingredients:
- 1 pound shrimp, peeled and deveined
- Salt and pepper to taste
- 2 tablespoons olive oil
- 1 teaspoon paprika
- 1 teaspoon garlic powder
- 1 avocado, diced
- 1 cup cherry tomatoes, halved
- 1/2 cucumber, diced
- 1/4 cup red onion, thinly sliced
- 1/4 cup chopped fresh cilantro or parsley
- Juice of 1 lime
- Optional: Mixed salad greens for serving

Instructions:
- Season the shrimp with salt, pepper, paprika, and garlic powder.

- Heat olive oil in a skillet over medium heat. Add the seasoned shrimp and cook for 2-3 minutes per side, or until they are pink and opaque. Remove from heat and let cool slightly.

- In a large bowl, combine the diced avocado, halved cherry tomatoes, diced cucumber, thinly sliced red onion, and chopped fresh cilantro or parsley.

- Add the cooked shrimp to the bowl with the other ingredients.

- Squeeze the lime juice over the salad and toss gently to combine.

- Taste and adjust seasoning if necessary.

- Serve the shrimp and avocado salad on a bed of mixed salad greens, if desired.

This shrimp and avocado salad is not only delicious and satisfying but also packed with protein, healthy fats, vitamins, and minerals. It's a light and refreshing dish that's perfect for a quick and easy lunch or dinner. Enjoy this wholesome and flavorful recipe!

89. Cauliflower Rice Sushi Rolls

Ingredients:
- 1 medium head cauliflower, grated or pulsed into rice-like texture
- 2 tablespoons rice vinegar
- 1 tablespoon sugar or sweetener of choice
- 1/2 teaspoon salt
- 4 nori seaweed sheets
- Assorted fillings: sliced cucumber, avocado, carrot sticks, bell pepper strips, cooked shrimp or crab, etc.
- Soy sauce or tamari, for serving
- Pickled ginger, for serving (optional)
- Wasabi, for serving (optional)

Instructions:
- In a small bowl, combine the rice vinegar, sugar, and salt. Stir until the sugar and salt are dissolved.

- Place the grated cauliflower in a microwave-safe bowl and microwave on high for 2-3 minutes, or until softened. Alternatively, you can sauté the cauliflower rice in a skillet over medium heat for 5-7 minutes until tender.

- Transfer the cooked cauliflower rice to a clean kitchen towel and squeeze out excess moisture.

- In a mixing bowl, combine the cauliflower rice with the rice vinegar mixture. Stir until well combined and let it cool slightly.

- Place a nori seaweed sheet shiny side down on a bamboo sushi rolling mat or a clean kitchen towel.

- Spread a thin layer of cauliflower rice evenly over the nori sheet, leaving about a half-inch border at the top edge.

- Arrange your desired fillings in a row along the bottom edge of the cauliflower rice-covered nori sheet.

- Starting from the bottom edge, tightly roll the nori sheet and cauliflower rice over the fillings, using the bamboo sushi rolling mat or kitchen towel to help shape and compress the roll.

- Continue rolling until you reach the top edge, sealing the edge with a little water if necessary. Repeat the process with the remaining nori sheets and fillings.

- Once all the rolls are assembled, use a sharp knife to slice each roll into 6-8 pieces. Serve the cauliflower rice sushi rolls with soy sauce or tamari for dipping, and pickled ginger and wasabi on the side, if desired.

90. Turkey Taco Lettuce Wraps

Ingredients:

- 1 tablespoon olive oil
- 1 pound lean ground turkey
- 1 small onion, diced
- 2 cloves garlic, minced
- 1 tablespoon chili powder
- 1 teaspoon ground cumin
- 1/2 teaspoon paprika
- 1/4 teaspoon dried oregano
- Salt and pepper to taste
- 1 cup diced tomatoes
- 1/2 cup tomato sauce
- 1/4 cup chopped fresh cilantro
- 1 tablespoon lime juice
- 1 head iceberg lettuce or butter lettuce, leaves separated
- Optional toppings: diced avocado, shredded cheese, salsa, Greek yogurt or sour cream, sliced jalapenos

Instructions:

- Heat olive oil in a large skillet over medium heat.

- Add the diced onion and minced garlic to the skillet. Cook for 2-3 minutes, or until softened and fragrant.

- Add the ground turkey to the skillet, breaking it up with a spoon. Cook for 5-7 minutes, or until browned and cooked through.

- Stir in the chili powder, ground cumin, paprika, dried oregano, salt, and pepper. Cook for another 2-3 minutes, or until the spices are fragrant.

- Add the diced tomatoes and tomato sauce to the skillet. Bring to a simmer and cook for 5-7 minutes, or until the sauce has thickened slightly.

- Remove from heat and stir in the chopped fresh cilantro and lime juice.

- To assemble the lettuce wraps, spoon the turkey taco mixture onto the center of each lettuce leaf.

- Top with your desired toppings, such as diced avocado, shredded cheese, salsa, Greek yogurt or sour cream, and sliced jalapenos. Serve immediately, and enjoy!

These turkey taco lettuce wraps are not only delicious and satisfying but also low in carbs and packed with protein, fiber, vitamins, and minerals. They make a perfect light and nutritious meal for lunch or dinner, and they're also great for those following a low-carb or gluten-free diet. Enjoy this wholesome and flavorful recipe!

91. Lentil and Kale Soup

Ingredients:
* 1 tablespoon olive oil
* 1 onion, chopped
* 2 carrots, chopped
* 2 celery stalks, chopped
* 3 cloves garlic, minced
* 1 cup dried green or brown lentils, rinsed
* 6 cups vegetable broth or chicken broth
* 1 can (14 oz) diced tomatoes
* 2 cups chopped kale leaves, tough stems removed
* 1 teaspoon dried thyme
* 1 teaspoon dried oregano
* Salt and pepper to taste
* Juice of 1 lemon
* Optional toppings: grated Parmesan cheese, chopped fresh parsley, red pepper flakes

Instructions:
* Heat olive oil in a large pot or Dutch oven over medium heat.

* Add the chopped onion, carrots, and celery to the pot. Cook for 5-7 minutes, or until the vegetables are softened.

* Add the minced garlic to the pot and cook for another minute, or until fragrant.

* Stir in the rinsed lentils, vegetable broth or chicken broth, diced tomatoes (with their juices), chopped kale leaves, dried thyme, and dried oregano.

* Bring the soup to a boil, then reduce the heat to low. Cover and simmer for 20-25 minutes, or until the lentils are tender.

* Season the soup with salt and pepper to taste. Stir in the lemon juice just before serving.

* Ladle the soup into bowls and top with optional toppings such as grated Parmesan cheese, chopped fresh parsley, and red pepper flakes, if desired. Serve hot and enjoy!

This lentil and kale soup is not only delicious and satisfying but also packed with protein, fiber, vitamins, and minerals. It's a comforting and nutritious meal that's perfect for chilly days or whenever you need a nourishing pick-me-up. Enjoy this wholesome and flavorful recipe!

92. Mediterranean Chickpea Quinoa Bowl

Ingredients:

- 1 cup quinoa, rinsed
- 2 cups vegetable broth or water
- 1 tablespoon olive oil
- 1 onion, diced
- 2 cloves garlic, minced
- 1 can (15 oz) chickpeas, drained and rinsed
- 1 teaspoon ground cumin
- 1 teaspoon paprika
- 1/2 teaspoon ground coriander
- Salt and pepper to taste
- 1 cup cherry tomatoes, halved
- 1/2 English cucumber, diced
- 1/4 cup Kalamata olives, sliced
- 1/4 cup crumbled feta cheese
- 2 tablespoons chopped fresh parsley
- Juice of 1 lemon
- Optional toppings: sliced avocado, hummus, tzatziki sauce

Instructions:

- In a medium saucepan, bring the vegetable broth or water to a boil. Add the quinoa, reduce the heat to low, cover, and simmer for 15-20 minutes, or until the quinoa is cooked and the liquid is absorbed. Remove from heat and let it sit, covered, for 5 minutes. Fluff with a fork and set aside.

- While the quinoa is cooking, heat olive oil in a large skillet over medium heat.

- Add the diced onion to the skillet and cook for 5-7 minutes, or until softened.

- Add the minced garlic to the skillet and cook for another minute, or until fragrant.

- Stir in the drained and rinsed chickpeas, ground cumin, paprika, ground coriander, salt, and pepper. Cook for 5-7 minutes, or until the chickpeas are heated through and lightly browned.

- In a large mixing bowl, combine the cooked quinoa, cooked chickpeas, halved cherry tomatoes, diced cucumber, sliced Kalamata olives, crumbled feta cheese, chopped fresh parsley, and lemon juice. Toss gently to combine.

- Divide the chickpea quinoa mixture among serving bowls.

- Top each bowl with optional toppings such as sliced avocado, hummus, or tzatziki sauce, if desired. Serve immediately, and enjoy!

These Mediterranean chickpea quinoa bowls are not only delicious and satisfying but also packed with protein, fiber, vitamins, and minerals. They make a perfect light and nutritious meal for lunch or dinner, and they're also great for meal prep. Enjoy this wholesome and flavorful recipe!

93. Lemon Herb Grilled Shrimp

Ingredients:
- 1 pound large shrimp, peeled and deveined
- Zest of 1 lemon
- Juice of 1 lemon
- 2 cloves garlic, minced
- 2 tablespoons chopped fresh parsley
- 1 tablespoon chopped fresh dill
- 1 tablespoon chopped fresh basil
- 2 tablespoons olive oil
- Salt and pepper to taste
- Wooden or metal skewers (if using wooden skewers, soak them in water for 30 minutes before grilling)

Instructions:

- In a large mixing bowl, combine the lemon zest, lemon juice, minced garlic, chopped fresh parsley, chopped fresh dill, chopped fresh basil, olive oil, salt, and pepper. Stir until well combined.

- Add the peeled and deveined shrimp to the bowl with the marinade. Toss to coat the shrimp evenly with the marinade. Cover the bowl and refrigerate for at least 30 minutes, or up to 2 hours.

- Preheat your grill to medium-high heat.

- Thread the marinated shrimp onto skewers, leaving a little space between each shrimp.

- Grill the shrimp skewers for 2-3 minutes per side, or until they are pink and opaque.

- Remove the shrimp skewers from the grill and transfer them to a serving platter.

- Serve the lemon herb grilled shrimp hot, garnished with additional chopped fresh herbs if desired. Enjoy!

These lemon herb grilled shrimp are not only delicious and satisfying but also packed with protein and healthy fats. They make a perfect main dish for a light and nutritious meal, and they're also great for outdoor grilling or entertaining. Enjoy this wholesome and flavorful recipe!

94. Veggie and Hummus Wrap

Ingredients:
- 4 large whole wheat or spinach tortillas
- 1 cup hummus (store-bought or homemade)
- 2 cups mixed salad greens
- 1 cucumber, thinly sliced
- 1 bell pepper (any color), thinly sliced
- 1 carrot, grated or thinly sliced
- 1/2 red onion, thinly sliced
- 1/4 cup chopped fresh herbs (such as parsley, cilantro, or basil)
- Salt and pepper to taste
- Optional additions: sliced avocado, shredded cheese, sun-dried tomatoes, sprouts

Instructions:
- Lay out the tortillas on a clean work surface.

- Spread about 1/4 cup of hummus evenly over each tortilla, leaving a small border around the edges.

- Layer the mixed salad greens, sliced cucumber, sliced bell pepper, grated carrot, and sliced red onion evenly over the hummus layer on each tortilla.

- Sprinkle the chopped fresh herbs over the vegetables.

- Season with salt and pepper to taste.

- If using any optional additions, such as sliced avocado, shredded cheese, sun-dried tomatoes, or sprouts, add them now.

- Fold the bottom edge of each tortilla up over the filling, then fold in the sides, and roll tightly to enclose the filling.

- Cut each wrap in half diagonally, if desired.

- Serve immediately, or wrap tightly in foil or plastic wrap for later.

These veggie and hummus wraps are not only delicious and satisfying but also packed with fiber, vitamins, and minerals. They make a perfect light and nutritious meal for lunch or dinner, and they're also great for meal prep or on-the-go eating. Enjoy this wholesome and flavorful recipe!

95. Baked Chicken Tenders with Honey Mustard

Ingredients:

- 1/2 teaspoon garlic powder
- 1/2 cup plain Greek yogurt
- 2 tablespoons Dijon mustard
- 2 tablespoons honey
- 1 tablespoon olive oil
- Fresh parsley or chives for garnish (optional)
- 1 pound chicken tenders or boneless, skinless chicken breasts, cut into strips
- Salt and pepper to taste
- 1 cup breadcrumbs (whole wheat or gluten-free)
- 1/4 cup grated Parmesan cheese (optional)
- 1 teaspoon paprika

Instructions:

- Preheat your oven to 400°F (200°C). Line a baking sheet with parchment paper or lightly grease it with olive oil.

- Season the chicken tenders with salt and pepper. In a shallow dish, combine the breadcrumbs, grated Parmesan cheese (if using), paprika, and garlic powder.

- In another shallow dish, whisk together the Greek yogurt, Dijon mustard, honey, and olive oil until smooth.

- Dip each chicken tender into the yogurt mixture, coating it evenly, then dredge it in the breadcrumb mixture, pressing gently to adhere the breadcrumbs.

- Place the coated chicken tenders on the prepared baking sheet.

- Bake in the preheated oven for 15-20 minutes, or until the chicken is cooked through and golden brown.

- While the chicken tenders are baking, you can prepare the honey mustard sauce by mixing together additional honey and mustard to taste.

- Once the chicken tenders are done, remove them from the oven and let them cool for a few minutes.

- Serve the baked chicken tenders with honey mustard sauce on the side for dipping. Garnish with fresh parsley or chives, if desired. Enjoy!

These baked chicken tenders with honey mustard are not only delicious and satisfying but also packed with protein and healthy fats. They make a perfect main dish for a light and nutritious meal, and they're also great for meal prep or serving as an appetizer for gatherings. Enjoy this wholesome and flavorful recipe!

96. Tofu and Vegetable Curry

Ingredients:
- 1 tablespoon coconut oil or olive oil
- 1 onion, chopped
- 2 cloves garlic, minced
- 1 tablespoon grated ginger
- 1 tablespoon curry powder
- 1 teaspoon ground turmeric
- 1 teaspoon ground cumin
- 1 teaspoon ground coriander
- 1/2 teaspoon ground cinnamon
- 1/4 teaspoon cayenne pepper
(optional, for extra heat)
- 1 block (14 oz) firm tofu, pressed and cubed
- 2 cups mixed vegetables (such as bell peppers, carrots, broccoli, and snow peas), chopped
- 1 can (14 oz) coconut milk
- 1 cup vegetable broth or water
- 2 tablespoons soy sauce or tamari
- 1 tablespoon maple syrup or coconut sugar (optional, for sweetness)
- Salt and pepper to taste
- Cooked rice or quinoa, for serving
- Fresh cilantro, chopped, for garnish
- Lime wedges, for serving

Instructions:
- Heat coconut oil or olive oil in a large skillet or pot over medium heat. Add the chopped onion to the skillet and cook for 5-7 minutes, or until softened.

- Add the minced garlic and grated ginger to the skillet and cook for another minute, or until fragrant.

- Stir in the curry powder, ground turmeric, ground cumin, ground coriander, ground cinnamon, and cayenne pepper (if using). Cook for 1-2 minutes, stirring constantly, until the spices are fragrant.

- Add the cubed tofu and chopped mixed vegetables to the skillet. Stir to coat them evenly with the spice mixture. Pour in the coconut milk and vegetable broth or water. Bring the mixture to a simmer.

- Reduce the heat to low and let the curry simmer for 15-20 minutes, or until the vegetables are tender and the sauce has thickened slightly.

- Stir in the soy sauce or tamari and maple syrup or coconut sugar (if using). Season with salt and pepper to taste.

- Remove from heat and serve the tofu and vegetable curry hot over cooked rice or quinoa.

- Garnish with chopped fresh cilantro and serve with lime wedges on the side for squeezing over the curry. Enjoy!

97. Greek Stuffed Zucchini Boats

Ingredients:

- 4 medium zucchini
- 1 tablespoon olive oil
- 1 small onion, finely chopped
- 2 cloves garlic, minced
- 1 red bell pepper, diced
- 1 cup cherry tomatoes, halved
- 1/4 cup chopped fresh parsley
- 2 tablespoons chopped fresh dill
- 1/4 cup pitted Kalamata olives, chopped
- Salt and pepper to taste
- 1/2 cup crumbled feta cheese
- Optional: Lemon wedges for serving

Instructions:

- Preheat your oven to 375°F (190°C). Grease a baking dish with olive oil or non-stick spray.

- Cut each zucchini in half lengthwise. Use a spoon to scoop out the flesh from the center of each zucchini half, leaving about a 1/4-inch thick shell. Chop the scooped-out zucchini flesh and set aside.

- Heat olive oil in a large skillet over medium heat. Add the chopped onion and minced garlic to the skillet and cook for 2-3 minutes, or until softened and fragrant. Add the diced red bell pepper to the skillet and cook for another 2-3 minutes.

- Add the chopped zucchini flesh and cherry tomatoes to the skillet. Cook for 5-7 minutes, or until the vegetables are softened.

- Remove the skillet from heat and stir in the crumbled feta cheese, chopped fresh parsley, chopped fresh dill, and chopped Kalamata olives. Season with salt and pepper to taste.

- Arrange the hollowed-out zucchini halves in the greased baking dish. Spoon the vegetable and feta mixture evenly into each zucchini boat.

- Cover the baking dish with foil and bake in the preheated oven for 20-25 minutes, or until the zucchini boats are tender.

- Remove the foil and bake for an additional 5 minutes, or until the tops are lightly browned. Serve the Greek stuffed zucchini boats hot, with lemon wedges on the side for squeezing over the top, if desired. Enjoy!

These Greek stuffed zucchini boats are not only delicious and satisfying but also packed with fiber, vitamins, and minerals. They make a perfect light and nutritious meal for lunch or dinner, and they're also great for meal prep. Enjoy this wholesome and flavorful recipe!

98. Quinoa and Black Bean Burrito Bowl

Ingredients:

- 1 cup quinoa, rinsed
- 2 cups vegetable broth or water
- 1 tablespoon olive oil
- 1 onion, chopped
- 2 cloves garlic, minced
- 1 bell pepper (any color), chopped
- 1 cup corn kernels

(fresh, canned, or frozen)

- 1 can (15 oz) black beans, drained and rinsed
- 1 teaspoon ground cumin
- 1 teaspoon chili powder
- Salt and pepper to taste
- Optional toppings: sliced avocado, diced tomatoes, shredded lettuce, chopped cilantro, salsa, Greek yogurt or sour cream, lime wedges

Instructions:

- In a medium saucepan, bring the vegetable broth or water to a boil. Add the quinoa, reduce the heat to low, cover, and simmer for 15-20 minutes, or until the quinoa is cooked and the liquid is absorbed. Remove from heat and let it sit, covered, for 5 minutes. Fluff with a fork and set aside.

- While the quinoa is cooking, heat olive oil in a large skillet over medium heat.

- Add the chopped onion to the skillet and cook for 5-7 minutes, or until softened.

- Add the minced garlic and chopped bell pepper to the skillet and cook for another 2-3 minutes.

- Stir in the corn kernels, black beans, ground cumin, and chili powder. Cook for 5-7 minutes, or until the vegetables are tender and the beans are heated through.

- Season with salt and pepper to taste. To assemble the burrito bowls, divide the cooked quinoa among serving bowls. Top each bowl with the black bean and vegetable mixture.

- Add your desired toppings, such as sliced avocado, diced tomatoes, shredded lettuce, chopped cilantro, salsa, Greek yogurt or sour cream, and lime wedges. Serve immediately, and enjoy!

These quinoa and black bean burrito bowls are not only delicious and satisfying but also packed with protein, fiber, vitamins, and minerals. They make a perfect light and nutritious meal for lunch or dinner, and they're also great for meal prep. Enjoy this wholesome and flavorful recipe!

99. Lemon Garlic Roast Pork Tenderloin

Ingredients:
- 1 pork tenderloin (about 1 to 1.5 pounds)
- Salt and pepper to taste
- 2 tablespoons olive oil
- 4 cloves garlic, minced
- Zest of 1 lemon
- Juice of 1 lemon
- 1 tablespoon chopped fresh rosemary (or 1 teaspoon dried rosemary)
- 1 tablespoon chopped fresh thyme (or 1 teaspoon dried thyme)
- 1 tablespoon honey (optional, for a touch of sweetness)

Instructions:
- Preheat your oven to 375°F (190°C).

- Pat the pork tenderloin dry with paper towels and season all over with salt and pepper.

- In a small bowl, mix together the olive oil, minced garlic, lemon zest, lemon juice, chopped fresh rosemary, chopped fresh thyme, and honey (if using).

- Rub the garlic and herb mixture all over the pork tenderloin, making sure it's evenly coated.

- Place the pork tenderloin in a roasting pan or on a baking sheet lined with parchment paper.

- Roast in the preheated oven for 25-30 minutes, or until the internal temperature reaches 145°F (63°C) for medium-rare or 160°F (71°C) for medium, as measured with a meat thermometer inserted into the thickest part of the tenderloin.

- Remove the pork tenderloin from the oven and let it rest for 5-10 minutes before slicing.

- Slice the pork tenderloin into medallions and serve with your favorite side dishes, such as roasted vegetables, steamed greens, or a fresh salad. Enjoy!

This lemon garlic roast pork tenderloin is not only delicious and satisfying but also packed with protein and essential nutrients. It makes a perfect main dish for a light and nutritious meal, and it's also great for meal prep. Enjoy this wholesome and flavorful recipe!

100. Thai Veggie Spring Rolls with Peanut Sauce

Ingredients:
For the Spring Rolls:
- 8 rice paper wrappers
- 2 cups mixed salad greens
- 1 cucumber, julienned
- 1 carrot, julienned
- 1 bell pepper (any color), thinly sliced
- 1 avocado, thinly sliced
- 1/4 cup fresh cilantro leaves
- 1/4 cup fresh mint leaves
- 1/4 cup fresh basil leaves
- Optional: cooked vermicelli noodles or tofu strips

For the Peanut Sauce:
- 1/4 cup creamy peanut butter
- 2 tablespoons soy sauce or tamari
- 1 tablespoon rice vinegar
- 1 tablespoon honey or maple syrup
- 1 teaspoon sesame oil
- 1 clove garlic, minced
- Water, as needed to thin the sauce

Instructions:
For the Spring Rolls:
- Prepare all the veggies and herbs for the filling and arrange them on a plate or cutting board.

- Fill a shallow dish with warm water. Working with one rice paper wrapper at a time, dip it into the warm water for about 10-15 seconds until it becomes soft and pliable.

- Carefully transfer the softened rice paper wrapper to a clean work surface.

- Place a small handful of mixed salad greens in the center of the wrapper, leaving some space around the edges.

- Layer the julienned cucumber, carrot, bell pepper, avocado slices, and fresh herbs on top of the salad greens.

- If using, add a small amount of cooked vermicelli noodles or tofu strips on top of the veggies.

- Fold the bottom edge of the rice paper wrapper over the filling, then fold in the sides, and roll tightly to form a spring roll.

- Repeat with the remaining rice paper wrappers and filling ingredients.

- Serve the spring rolls immediately, or store them in an airtight container in the refrigerator for up to 1 day. Serve with peanut sauce for dipping.

For the Peanut Sauce:

- In a small bowl, whisk together the creamy peanut butter, soy sauce or tamari, rice vinegar, honey or maple syrup, sesame oil, and minced garlic until smooth.

- If the sauce is too thick, add water, 1 tablespoon at a time, until desired consistency is reached.

- Serve the peanut sauce with the Thai veggie spring rolls for dipping.

These Thai veggie spring rolls with peanut sauce are not only delicious and satisfying but also packed with fiber, vitamins, and minerals. They make a perfect light and nutritious meal or snack, and they're also great for meal prep or serving at gatherings. Enjoy this wholesome and flavorful recipe!

101. Turkey and Vegetable Stir-Fry

Ingredients:

- 1 pound turkey breast or turkey tenderloin, thinly sliced
- 2 tablespoons soy sauce or tamari
- 1 tablespoon rice vinegar
- 1 tablespoon honey or maple syrup
- 1 tablespoon sesame oil
- 2 cloves garlic, minced
- 1 teaspoon grated ginger
- 2 tablespoons olive oil or vegetable oil, divided
- 1 onion, thinly sliced
- 2 bell peppers (any color), thinly sliced
- 2 cups broccoli florets
- 1 cup snap peas or snow peas, trimmed
- Salt and pepper to taste
- Cooked rice or noodles, for serving
- Optional garnish: sesame seeds, chopped green onions

Instructions:

- In a bowl, combine the thinly sliced turkey with soy sauce or tamari, rice vinegar, honey or maple syrup, sesame oil, minced garlic, and grated ginger. Allow the turkey to marinate for at least 15-20 minutes, or refrigerate for up to 1 hour for best flavor.

- Heat 1 tablespoon of olive oil or vegetable oil in a large skillet or wok over medium-high heat. Add the marinated turkey slices to the skillet and stir-fry for 4-5 minutes, or until cooked through. Remove the cooked turkey from the skillet and set aside.

- In the same skillet, add the remaining tablespoon of oil.

- Add the thinly sliced onion and bell peppers to the skillet and stir-fry for 2-3 minutes, or until they start to soften.

- Add the broccoli florets and snap peas or snow peas to the skillet. Stir-fry for an additional 3-4 minutes, or until the vegetables are tender-crisp.

- Return the cooked turkey to the skillet and toss with the vegetables. Season with salt and pepper to taste.

- Serve the turkey and vegetable stir-fry hot over cooked rice or noodles. Garnish with sesame seeds and chopped green onions, if desired. Enjoy!

This turkey and vegetable stir-fry is not only delicious and satisfying but also packed with protein, fiber, vitamins, and minerals. It makes a perfect light and nutritious meal for lunch or dinner, and it's also great for meal prep. Enjoy this wholesome and flavorful recipe!

102. Mediterranean Baked Cod

Ingredients:
- 4 cod fillets (about 6 oz each)
- Salt and pepper to taste
- 2 tablespoons olive oil
- 4 cloves garlic, minced
- 1 pint cherry tomatoes, halved
- 1/4 cup Kalamata olives, pitted and halved
- 2 tablespoons capers, drained
- 1 teaspoon dried oregano
- 1 teaspoon dried basil
- 1/2 teaspoon dried thyme
- Juice of 1 lemon
- Fresh parsley, chopped, for garnish

Instructions:
- Preheat your oven to 400°F (200°C). Grease a baking dish with olive oil or non-stick spray.

- Pat the cod fillets dry with paper towels and season both sides with salt and pepper.

- Place the seasoned cod fillets in the prepared baking dish.

- In a skillet, heat the olive oil over medium heat. Add the minced garlic and cook for 1-2 minutes, or until fragrant.

- Add the halved cherry tomatoes, halved Kalamata olives, drained capers, dried oregano, dried basil, and dried thyme to the skillet. Cook for 5-7 minutes, or until the tomatoes start to soften and release their juices.

- Pour the tomato mixture over the cod fillets in the baking dish.

- Squeeze the lemon juice over the cod fillets and tomato mixture.

- Cover the baking dish with foil and bake in the preheated oven for 15-20 minutes, or until the cod is cooked through and flakes easily with a fork.

- Remove the foil and bake for an additional 5 minutes, or until the top is lightly browned.
- Remove from the oven and let it rest for a few minutes.

- Garnish with chopped fresh parsley before serving. Enjoy!

This Mediterranean baked cod is not only delicious and satisfying but also packed with protein, healthy fats, and antioxidants. It makes a perfect main dish for a light and nutritious meal, and it's also great for meal prep. Enjoy this wholesome and flavorful recipe!

103. Spinach and Feta Stuffed Portobello Mushrooms

Ingredients:

- 1/4 cup crumbled feta cheese
- 1/4 cup grated Parmesan cheese
- Salt and pepper to taste
- Fresh parsley, chopped, for garnish
- 4 large portobello mushrooms, stems removed
- 2 tablespoons olive oil
- 2 cloves garlic, minced
- 4 cups fresh spinach leaves

Instructions:

- Preheat your oven to 375°F (190°C). Line a baking sheet with parchment paper.

- Clean the portobello mushrooms by wiping them with a damp paper towel. Carefully remove the stems and scoop out the gills with a spoon to create a hollow cavity in each mushroom cap.

- In a large skillet, heat the olive oil over medium heat. Add the minced garlic and cook for 1-2 minutes, or until fragrant.

- Add the fresh spinach leaves to the skillet and cook, stirring occasionally, until wilted, about 2-3 minutes.

- Remove the skillet from heat and let the spinach cool slightly. Once cooled, chop the spinach into smaller pieces.

- In a mixing bowl, combine the chopped spinach, crumbled feta cheese, grated Parmesan cheese, and salt and pepper to taste. Mix until well combined.

- Spoon the spinach and feta mixture evenly into the hollowed-out portobello mushroom caps, pressing down gently to pack the filling. Place the stuffed portobello mushrooms on the prepared baking sheet.

- Bake in the preheated oven for 15-20 minutes, or until the mushrooms are tender and the filling is heated through.

- Remove from the oven and let them cool for a few minutes before serving. Garnish with chopped fresh parsley before serving. Enjoy!

These spinach and feta stuffed portobello mushrooms are not only delicious and satisfying but also packed with fiber, vitamins, and minerals. They make a perfect appetizer or side dish for a light and nutritious meal, and they're also great for meal prep. Enjoy this wholesome and flavorful recipe!

104. Ratatouille Stuffed Bell Peppers

Ingredients:

- 1 yellow squash, diced
- 1 red bell pepper, diced
- 1 can (14 oz) diced tomatoes
- 1 teaspoon dried thyme
- 1 teaspoon dried oregano
- Salt and pepper to taste
- 1/4 cup chopped fresh basil, for garnish
- 4 large bell peppers (any color), halved and seeds removed
- 2 tablespoons olive oil
- 1 onion, diced
- 2 cloves garlic, minced
- 1 eggplant, diced
- 1 zucchini, diced

Instructions:

- Preheat your oven to 375Â°F (190Â°C). Grease a baking dish with olive oil or non-stick spray.

- Heat the olive oil in a large skillet over medium heat. Add the diced onion and minced garlic and cook until softened, about 5 minutes.

- Add the diced eggplant, zucchini, yellow squash, and red bell pepper to the skillet. Cook until the vegetables are tender, about 10 minutes.

- Stir in the diced tomatoes, dried thyme, dried oregano, salt, and pepper. Cook for an additional 5 minutes, allowing the flavors to meld together.

- While the ratatouille mixture is cooking, prepare the bell peppers by halving them and removing the seeds. Place them in the greased baking dish.

- Spoon the ratatouille mixture into each bell pepper half, pressing down gently to fill.

- Cover the baking dish with foil and bake in the preheated oven for 30-35 minutes, or until the bell peppers are tender.

- Remove the foil and bake for an additional 5-10 minutes to allow the tops to brown slightly.

- Remove from the oven and let cool for a few minutes before serving. Garnish with chopped fresh basil before serving. Enjoy!

These ratatouille stuffed bell peppers are not only delicious and satisfying but also packed with fiber, vitamins, and minerals. They make a perfect light and nutritious meal for lunch or dinner, and they're also great for meal prep. Enjoy this wholesome and flavorful recipe!

105. Quinoa Salad with Roasted Chickpeas

Ingredients:

For the Quinoa Salad:
- 1 cup quinoa, rinsed
- 2 cups water or vegetable broth
- 1 can (15 oz) chickpeas, drained and rinsed
- 2 tablespoons olive oil
- 1 teaspoon ground cumin
- 1 teaspoon smoked paprika
- Salt and pepper to taste
- 1 cucumber, diced
- 1 bell pepper (any color), diced
- 1 cup cherry tomatoes, halved
- 1/4 cup chopped fresh parsley
- 1/4 cup chopped fresh mint
- 1/4 cup crumbled feta cheese (optional)

For the Dressing:
- 1/4 cup olive oil
- 2 tablespoons lemon juice
- 1 teaspoon Dijon mustard
- 1 clove garlic, minced
- Salt and pepper to taste

Instructions:

For the Quinoa Salad:
- Preheat your oven to 400Â°F (200Â°C). Line a baking sheet with parchment paper.

- In a medium saucepan, combine the quinoa and water or vegetable broth. Bring to a boil, then reduce the heat to low, cover, and simmer for 15-20 minutes, or until the quinoa is cooked and the liquid is absorbed. Remove from heat and let it cool.

- Meanwhile, pat the drained and rinsed chickpeas dry with paper towels. In a bowl, toss the chickpeas with olive oil, ground cumin, smoked paprika, salt, and pepper until evenly coated. Spread the chickpeas in a single layer on the prepared baking sheet.

- Roast the chickpeas in the preheated oven for 20-25 minutes, or until crispy, shaking the pan halfway through cooking. In a large bowl, combine the cooked quinoa, diced cucumber, diced bell pepper, halved cherry tomatoes, chopped fresh parsley, and chopped fresh mint.

- Add the roasted chickpeas to the bowl and toss to combine. If using, sprinkle the crumbled feta cheese over the salad. Set aside while you prepare the dressing.

For the Dressing:
- In a small bowl, whisk together the olive oil, lemon juice, Dijon mustard, minced garlic, salt, and pepper until well combined. Pour the dressing over the quinoa salad and toss to coat evenly.

- Taste and adjust seasoning, if necessary. Serve the quinoa salad immediately, or refrigerate for at least 30 minutes to allow the flavors to meld together. Enjoy!

106. Lemon Herb Grilled Chicken Skewers

Ingredients:

- 1.5 lbs boneless, skinless chicken breasts, cut into cubes
- Zest and juice of 1 lemon
- 2 tablespoons olive oil
- 2 cloves garlic, minced
- 1 tablespoon fresh thyme leaves (or 1 teaspoon dried thyme)
- 1 tablespoon fresh rosemary leaves (or 1 teaspoon dried rosemary)
- Salt and pepper to taste
- Wooden skewers, soaked in water for at least 30 minutes

Instructions:

- In a large bowl, combine the lemon zest, lemon juice, olive oil, minced garlic, fresh thyme leaves, fresh rosemary leaves, salt, and pepper. Mix well to make the marinade.

- Add the cubed chicken breast to the marinade and toss until evenly coated. Cover the bowl and marinate the chicken in the refrigerator for at least 30 minutes, or up to 4 hours for maximum flavor.

- Preheat your grill to medium-high heat.

- Thread the marinated chicken cubes onto the soaked wooden skewers, leaving a little space between each piece.

- Place the skewers on the preheated grill and cook for 8-10 minutes, turning occasionally, until the chicken is cooked through and has grill marks on all sides.

- Remove the chicken skewers from the grill and let them rest for a few minutes before serving.

- Serve the lemon herb grilled chicken skewers hot with your favorite side dishes, such as grilled vegetables, rice, or a fresh salad. Enjoy!

These lemon herb grilled chicken skewers are not only delicious and satisfying but also packed with protein and aromatic herbs. They make a perfect main dish for a light and nutritious meal, and they're also great for outdoor gatherings or barbecue parties. Enjoy this wholesome and flavorful recipe!

107. Tofu and Broccoli Stir-Fry

Ingredients:

- 14 oz (400g) firm tofu, pressed and cubed
- 2 tablespoons soy sauce or tamari
- 1 tablespoon rice vinegar
- 1 tablespoon honey or maple syrup
- 1 tablespoon sesame oil
- 2 cloves garlic, minced
- 1 teaspoon grated ginger
- 2 tablespoons olive oil or vegetable oil, divided
- 1 head broccoli, cut into florets
- 1 bell pepper, thinly sliced
- 1 carrot, thinly sliced
- 1/4 cup chopped green onions (scallions), for garnish
- Cooked rice or noodles, for serving

Instructions:

- In a small bowl, whisk together the soy sauce or tamari, rice vinegar, honey or maple syrup, sesame oil, minced garlic, and grated ginger to make the sauce.

- Heat 1 tablespoon of olive oil or vegetable oil in a large skillet or wok over medium-high heat.

- Add the cubed tofu to the skillet and cook for 5-7 minutes, or until golden brown on all sides. Remove the tofu from the skillet and set aside.

- In the same skillet, add the remaining tablespoon of oil.

- Add the broccoli florets, thinly sliced bell pepper, and thinly sliced carrot to the skillet. Stir-fry for 5-7 minutes, or until the vegetables are tender-crisp.

- Return the cooked tofu to the skillet and pour the sauce over the tofu and vegetables. Stir to coat everything evenly with the sauce.

- Cook for an additional 2-3 minutes, or until the sauce has thickened slightly. Remove from heat and garnish with chopped green onions (scallions). Serve the tofu and broccoli stir-fry hot over cooked rice or noodles. Enjoy!

This tofu and broccoli stir-fry is not only delicious and satisfying but also packed with protein, fiber, vitamins, and minerals. It makes a perfect light and nutritious meal for lunch or dinner, and it's also great for meal prep. Enjoy this wholesome and flavorful recipe!

108. Greek Shrimp Orzo Salad

Ingredients:

- 8 oz (about 225g) orzo pasta
- 1 lb (about 450g) shrimp, peeled and deveined
- 2 tablespoons olive oil, divided
- 2 cloves garlic, minced
- 1 teaspoon dried oregano
- Salt and pepper to taste
- Juice of 1 lemon
- 1 cup cherry tomatoes, halved
- 1 cucumber, diced
- 1/2 red onion, thinly sliced
- 1/4 cup Kalamata olives, pitted and halved
- 1/4 cup crumbled feta cheese
- 2 tablespoons chopped fresh parsley, for garnish
- Optional: sliced grilled bell peppers or artichoke hearts
- For the Greek Dressing:
- 1/4 cup olive oil
- 2 tablespoons red wine vinegar
- 1 teaspoon Dijon mustard
- 1 teaspoon dried oregano
- 1 clove garlic, minced
- Salt and pepper to taste

Instructions:

- Cook the orzo pasta according to the package instructions until al dente. Drain and rinse under cold water to cool. Set aside.

- In a bowl, toss the shrimp with 1 tablespoon of olive oil, minced garlic, dried oregano, salt, pepper, and lemon juice until evenly coated.

- Heat the remaining tablespoon of olive oil in a skillet over medium-high heat. Add the shrimp and cook for 2-3 minutes per side, or until pink and cooked through. Remove from heat and let cool slightly.

- In a large bowl, combine the cooked orzo pasta, cooked shrimp, halved cherry tomatoes, diced cucumber, thinly sliced red onion, halved Kalamata olives, crumbled feta cheese, and optional sliced grilled bell peppers or artichoke hearts.

- In a small bowl, whisk together the ingredients for the Greek dressing: olive oil, red wine vinegar, Dijon mustard, dried oregano, minced garlic, salt, and pepper.

- Pour the Greek dressing over the salad and toss to coat everything evenly.

- Garnish the Greek shrimp orzo salad with chopped fresh parsley before serving. Serve chilled or at room temperature. Enjoy!

This Greek shrimp orzo salad is not only delicious and satisfying but also packed with protein, fiber, vitamins, and minerals. It makes a perfect light and nutritious meal for lunch or dinner, and it's also great for picnics or potlucks. Enjoy this wholesome and flavorful recipe!

109. Veggie and Bean Enchiladas

Ingredients:

For the Enchilada Filling:

- 1 tablespoon olive oil
- 1 onion, diced
- 2 cloves garlic, minced
- 1 bell pepper, diced
- 1 zucchini, diced
- 1 cup corn kernels (fresh, frozen, or canned)
- 1 can (15 oz) black beans, drained and rinsed
- 1 teaspoon ground cumin
- 1 teaspoon chili powder
- Salt and pepper to taste
- 1/4 cup chopped fresh cilantro

For the Enchilada Sauce:

- 2 tablespoons olive oil
- 2 tablespoons all-purpose flour (or gluten-free flour)
- 2 tablespoons chili powder
- 1 teaspoon ground cumin
- 1/2 teaspoon garlic powder
- 1/4 teaspoon dried oregano
- 2 cups vegetable broth
- Salt and pepper to taste

For Assembling:

- 8 small corn or flour tortillas
- 1 cup shredded cheese (cheddar, Monterey Jack, or Mexican blend)
- Optional toppings: chopped fresh cilantro, diced avocado, sliced green onions, sour cream or Greek yogurt

Instructions:

For the Enchilada Filling:

- Heat 1 tablespoon of olive oil in a large skillet over medium heat. Add the diced onion and cook until softened, about 5 minutes.

- Add the minced garlic, diced bell pepper, diced zucchini, and corn kernels to the skillet. Cook for another 5 minutes, or until the vegetables are tender.

- Stir in the black beans, ground cumin, chili powder, salt, and pepper. Cook for an additional 2-3 minutes to heat through.

- Remove the skillet from the heat and stir in the chopped fresh cilantro. Set aside.

For the Enchilada Sauce:
- In a medium saucepan, heat 2 tablespoons of olive oil over medium heat.

- Stir in the all-purpose flour and cook for 1 minute, stirring constantly.

- Add the chili powder, ground cumin, garlic powder, dried oregano, salt, and pepper. Cook for another minute, stirring constantly.

- Gradually whisk in the vegetable broth until smooth. Bring the sauce to a simmer and cook for 5-7 minutes, or until thickened. Remove from heat and set aside.

For Assembling:
- Preheat your oven to 375Â°F (190Â°C). Grease a 9x13-inch baking dish.

- Spread a thin layer of enchilada sauce on the bottom of the prepared baking dish.

- Warm the tortillas according to package instructions to make them pliable.

- Spoon some of the veggie and bean filling onto each tortilla, then roll them up tightly and place them seam side down in the baking dish.

- Pour the remaining enchilada sauce over the rolled tortillas, spreading it evenly to cover.

- Sprinkle shredded cheese over the top of the enchiladas.

- Cover the baking dish with foil and bake in the preheated oven for 20-25 minutes, or until the enchiladas are heated through and the cheese is melted.

- Remove the foil and bake for an additional 5 minutes, or until the cheese is bubbly and lightly browned.

- Remove from the oven and let cool for a few minutes before serving.

- Serve the veggie and bean enchiladas hot, garnished with chopped fresh cilantro, diced avocado, sliced green onions, and sour cream or Greek yogurt, if desired. Enjoy!

These veggie and bean enchiladas are not only delicious and satisfying but also packed with fiber, vitamins, and minerals. They make a perfect vegetarian meal for lunch or dinner, and they're also great for meal prep. Enjoy this wholesome and flavorful recipe!

110. Stuffed Cabbage Rolls with Ground Turkey and Rice

Ingredients:

For the Cabbage Rolls:
- 1 large head of cabbage
- 1 lb (about 450g) lean ground turkey
- 1 cup cooked rice (white or brown)
- 1 onion, finely chopped
- 2 cloves garlic, minced
- 1 carrot, grated
- 1/4 cup chopped fresh parsley
- 1 teaspoon dried thyme
- Salt and pepper to taste
- 1 can (14 oz) diced tomatoes
- 1 can (8 oz) tomato sauce
- 1 tablespoon olive oil

Instructions:
- Preheat your oven to 375°F (190°C). Grease a 9x13-inch baking dish with olive oil or non-stick spray.

- Bring a large pot of salted water to a boil. Carefully remove the core from the cabbage head and place the whole cabbage in the boiling water. Cook for 5-7 minutes, or until the outer leaves are tender and can be easily peeled off. Remove the cabbage from the water and let it cool slightly.

- While the cabbage is cooling, prepare the filling. In a large skillet, heat the olive oil over medium heat. Add the chopped onion and minced garlic and cook until softened, about 5 minutes.

- Add the ground turkey to the skillet and cook, breaking it apart with a spatula, until browned and cooked through.

- Stir in the cooked rice, grated carrot, chopped parsley, dried thyme, salt, and pepper. Cook for another 2-3 minutes to allow the flavors to meld together. Remove from heat and let cool slightly.

- Carefully peel off the tender outer leaves of the cabbage, being careful not to tear them. Trim the tough rib from the base of each leaf.

- Place a spoonful of the turkey and rice filling onto the center of each cabbage leaf. Roll up the leaf, tucking in the sides as you go, to form a neat roll.

- Place the cabbage rolls seam side down in the prepared baking dish, arranging them snugly next to each other.

- In a bowl, mix together the diced tomatoes and tomato sauce. Pour the tomato mixture over the cabbage rolls, covering them evenly.

- Cover the baking dish with foil and bake in the preheated oven for 45-50 minutes, or until the cabbage rolls are tender.

- Remove the foil and bake for an additional 10-15 minutes, or until the tops are lightly browned.

- Remove from the oven and let cool for a few minutes before serving.

- Serve the stuffed cabbage rolls hot, garnished with additional chopped parsley if desired. Enjoy!

These stuffed cabbage rolls with ground turkey and rice are not only delicious and satisfying but also packed with protein, fiber, vitamins, and minerals. They make a perfect wholesome meal for lunch or dinner, and they're also great for meal prep. Enjoy this flavorful and comforting recipe!

*As we reach the end of **"The ADHD Cookbook for Women: 100+ ADHD Cookbook Recipes for Nourishing Meals,"** I hope this journey through the world of ADHD-friendly cooking has left you feeling inspired, empowered, and satisfied.*

Throughout this cookbook, we've explored the intersection of ADHD and nutrition, discovering how simple changes in diet can have a profound impact on managing symptoms and enhancing overall well-being. From nutrient-dense ingredients to mindful cooking techniques, each recipe has been carefully crafted to support women with ADHD on their journey to a healthier, more balanced life.

But beyond the recipes themselves, we've also delved into the broader themes of self-care, organization, and mindfulness in the kitchen. By cultivating an environment of intentionality and compassion, we can transform mealtime into a nourishing ritual—one that nourishes not only our bodies but also our souls.

As you continue on your culinary journey, I encourage you to experiment, adapt, and make these recipes your own. Use them as a springboard for creativity, and don't be afraid to try new flavors and ingredients. Remember, cooking is not just about feeding the body—it's about feeding the spirit, too.

I want to express my deepest gratitude to you, the reader, for entrusting me with your time and your appetite. It has been an honor to accompany you on this culinary adventure, and I hope that "The ADHD Cookbook for Women" will continue to serve as a source of inspiration and nourishment for years to come.

So, until we meet again in the kitchen, remember to savor each bite, embrace the joy of cooking, and above all, nourish yourself with love and kindness.

Bon appétit!

www.ingramcontent.com/pod-product-compliance
Lightning Source LLC
Chambersburg PA
CBHW081550250726
48653CB00009B/3365

9798327603486